AI skills beco

CW01429913

AI

CHATGPT ESSENTIALS
FROM NOVICE TO EXPERT

Written by
Obruche Orugbo, PhD

Copyright © 2024
Obruche Orugbo, PhD | Wells & Lake Publishing

All rights reserved. No part of this book may be reproduced,
stored in a retrieval system, or transmitted in any form or by
any means—electronic, mechanical, photocopying, recording,
or otherwise—without the prior written permission of the
publisher, except for brief quotations in critical reviews or
articles.

DISCLAIMER

The information provided in this book is intended to be educational and informative. While every effort has been made to ensure the accuracy of the content, the author and publisher assume no responsibility for errors, omissions, or inaccuracies. The reader should consult professional sources when using artificial intelligence technologies, especially in critical or sensitive environments. AI is an evolving field, and practices may change as advancements occur.

DEDICATION

To all the curious minds eager to explore the potential of AI. This book is dedicated to those who embrace learning, innovation, and the endless possibilities of technology.Acknowledgments

I would like to express my gratitude to the incredible team of AI researchers, developers, and educators who have contributed to advancing the field of artificial intelligence. Special thanks to the OpenAI team for their groundbreaking work on ChatGPT, which has inspired this journey. To my friends, colleagues, and family— thank you for your unwavering support, insights, and encouragement throughout this process. Lastly, to the readers: your passion for learning drives this work forward.

PREFACE

In a world where technology is constantly evolving, artificial intelligence has become a critical tool for innovation, problem-solving, and creativity. This book was written to provide you with a comprehensive understanding of ChatGPT, an AI model that transforms how we interact with machines. Whether you are just starting out or seeking to refine your skills, *AI ChatGPT Essentials - From Novice to Expert* will guide you through every step, from fundamental concepts to advanced techniques. My hope is that by the end of this book, you feel empowered to leverage AI in meaningful ways, transforming ideas into action.

Table of Contents

AI skills become the new table stakes

"To secure your career, mastering AI is essential; those who don't will inevitably be outpaced by those who do."

Obruche Orugbo, PhD.

CHAPTER 1
INTRODUCTION

Understanding Artificial intelligence

AT A GLANCE

This chapter provides a comprehensive introduction to AI, setting the stage for more detailed discussions on ChatGPT and its functionalities.

Artificial Intelligence (AI) stands at the forefront of technological innovation, reshaping industries, enhancing personal and professional lives, and pushing the boundaries of what machines can achieve. This chapter serves as an introduction to AI, exploring its definition, history, types, and applications, laying the groundwork for understanding the essential role AI plays in modern technology and society.

WHAT IS AI?

Artificial Intelligence, commonly abbreviated as AI, refers to the simulation of human intelligence processes by machines, particularly computer systems. These processes include learning (the acquisition of information and rules for using the information), reasoning (using the rules to reach approximate or definite conclusions), and self-correction.

AI aims to enable machines to perform tasks that typically require human intelligence, such as visual perception, speech recognition, decision-making, and language translation.

So here is a simple define to help you explain what AI is to anybody.

Imagine you have a very clever child, like one who can learn things by seeing you do them. AI is like that, but for computers. It's like showing your child how to bake a cake, and then they can start figuring out how to make cookies or muffins on their own.

Normally, we tell computers exactly what to do, step-by-step. With AI, we can give them a bunch of information and let them learn for themselves.

Artificial intelligence can be categorised into different types based on its capabilities and functionalities.

1. Narrow AI (Weak AI): This type of AI is designed to perform a narrow task or a specific set of tasks. Examples include speech recognition systems like Siri or Alexa, recommendation systems like those used by Netflix or Amazon, and autonomous vehicles.

2. General AI (Strong AI): This type of AI would be able to think and learn like a human. It could do anything a person can do intellectually, like reasoning, solving problems, and learning in various areas. This kind of AI does not exist yet and is still being researched.

3. Superintelligent AI: This refers to AI that surpasses human intelligence in every way, potentially leading to abilities and knowledge far beyond human comprehension. This concept is also speculative and primarily explored in theoretical discussions.

As for ChatGPT, it falls under the category of Narrow AI. Specifically, ChatGPT is a language model designed to understand and generate human-like text based on the input it receives. It can engage in conversations, answer questions, provide explanations, and generate text in a coherent manner. However, its capabilities are limited to processing and generating text and do not extend to other tasks or domains beyond language understanding and generation.

The term "ChatGPT" itself stands for "Chat Generative Pre-trained Transformers." It's a name that highlights its purpose as a chatbot (Chat) powered by a type of neural network architecture known as Transformer, which has been pre-trained on vast amounts of text data to generate human-like responses. This is why it is also refers to as Generative.

ChatGPT, like many AI systems today, is impressive in its ability to understand and generate human-like text. However, it's not considered a General AI, or Strong AI. Here's why:

Narrow Focus: ChatGPT is designed to perform specific tasks within a defined scope. It can generate text based on patterns in data but doesn't truly understand the meaning behind words. It's great at simulating conversation or providing information based on its training but lacks real comprehension or awareness.

No Self-Understanding: General AI would have self-awareness and the ability to understand and reason like a human across various contexts. ChatGPT, on the other hand, doesn't possess self-awareness. It can't reflect on its own thoughts or experiences because it doesn't have them—it's just a tool for processing and generating language.

Lacks Deep Reasoning: While ChatGPT can mimic reasoning by following patterns in the data it was trained on, it doesn't actually reason or think independently. It can't solve new, complex problems outside its training without guidance. General AI would be capable of independent problem-solving and adapting to new, unseen challenges, something ChatGPT isn't equipped to do.

Dependent on Training Data: ChatGPT relies entirely on the data it was trained on. It doesn't learn or improve on its own over time through experiences. Instead, it remains static until updated with new data by its developers. General AI would continuously learn and evolve from interactions and experiences, growing its knowledge and capabilities much like a human does.

No Physical World Interaction: General AI would interact with and understand the physical world. ChatGPT lacks this ability. It operates solely in the digital world, handling text input and output. It doesn't have senses or the ability to perceive and act in the physical environment, which limits its understanding and capabilities compared to what would be expected from General AI.

Limited Context Understanding: ChatGPT can handle specific contexts well, such as answering questions or generating text based on a given prompt. However, it struggles with maintaining long-term context in a conversation and can't apply knowledge flexibly across different topics. General AI would maintain a deep and flexible understanding across various contexts and adapt its knowledge appropriately.
So, while ChatGPT is a powerful tool for generating text and handling specific tasks, it lacks the broad, adaptable intelligence that characterizes General AI. It doesn't understand or reason like a human, can't learn from

experience independently, and is limited to operating within the confines of its training data and programming.

Also, AI can be categorized based on functionality and capabilities, such as reactive machines, limited memory, theory of mind and self-aware AI. Let me explain them briefly before delving deeper into a brief History of AI

How Generative AI Differs from Other AI Types

Generative AI creates new content, such as text, images, videos, or music. Unlike other AI types, which focus on analyzing or classifying existing data, generative AI's main job is to produce new material.

In the AI world, there are various types designed for different tasks:
Reactive Machines: Used in self driving cars.
Limited Memory AI: Helps forecast the weather.
Theory of Mind AI: Powers virtual customer assistants.
Narrow AI: Provides personalized product recommendations.
Supervised Learning: Identifies objects in images and videos.
Unsupervised Learning: Detects fraudulent bank transactions.
Reinforcement Learning: Teaches machines to play games.

Generative AI can sometimes fit into these categories, but its primary goal is to generate new content, unlike other AIs that might do so as a byproduct of their main function.

Now that we know where generative AI stands, let's dive deeper a little bit.

Reactive Machines

Reactive machines are the most basic type of AI systems that perceive the world directly and react to stimuli without storing memories or past experiences. They do not have the capability to learn from previous interactions. IBM's Deep Blue is an example of a reactive machine that evaluates all possible moves in a game of chess and selects the best one.

Limited Memory

Limited memory AI systems can store previous data and predictions when gathering information and weighing potential decisions. They use historical data to make better predictions. Most modern AI systems, like self-driving cars, use limited memory to observe the environment, such as traffic signals and the behavior of other vehicles, to make decisions.

Theory of Mind

This category is still theoretical and not yet realized. Theory of mind AI involves understanding that other entities have their own beliefs, desires, and intentions that influence their behavior. This type of AI aims to interact more naturally and humanely by understanding and predicting others' actions and emotions.

Self-Aware AI

Self-aware AI represents the future and ultimate stage of AI development. These AI systems have a sense of self, consciousness, and the ability to think and reason independently. Such systems are purely speculative at this point and remain a topic of philosophical and ethical debate. Now that we know where generative AI stands, let's dive into the history

BRIEF HISTORY OF AI

The history of AI is a fascinating journey from philosophical inquiry to practical technology. Key milestones in the development of AI include:

Early Foundations (1940s-1950s)

1943: Warren McCulloch and Walter Pitts published a paper on neural networks, proposing a model of artificial neurons, laying the groundwork for neural networks.

1950: Alan Turing, a British mathematician, introduced the concept of the Turing Test to determine a machine's ability to exhibit intelligent behavior equivalent to, or indistinguishable from, that of a human.

The Birth of AI (1956-1970s)

1956: The term "Artificial Intelligence" was coined by John McCarthy at the Dartmouth Conference, marking the official birth of AI as a field of study.

1966: ELIZA, an early natural language processing program created by Joseph Weizenbaum, demonstrated the ability to converse with humans using a simple script.

AI Winter and Resurgence (1970s-1990s)

1970s-1980s: The AI field experienced its first "AI Winter," a period of reduced funding and interest due to unmet expectations. Researchers faced challenges in scaling AI and dealing with complex problems.

1997: IBM's Deep Blue defeated world chess champion Garry Kasparov, marking a significant achievement in AI.

Modern AI (2000s-Present)

2011: IBM's Watson won the quiz show Jeopardy!, demonstrating the potential of AI in natural language understanding and information retrieval.

2016: Google DeepMind's AlphaGo defeated world champion Go player Lee Sedol, showcasing advances in deep learning and reinforcement learning.

APPLICATIONS OF AI

AI has found applications across various domains, significantly transforming industries and enhancing efficiency. Here are some notable examples:

Healthcare

AI is revolutionizing healthcare through applications such as: Medical Imaging: AI algorithms assist in diagnosing diseases from imaging data, such as X-rays and MRIs, by detecting patterns that may be invisible to the human eye.

Predictive Analytics: AI predicts patient outcomes, potential diseases, and treatment success by analyzing medical records and data patterns.

Robotic Surgery: AI-powered robotic systems perform complex surgeries with precision, reducing recovery times and improving patient outcomes.

Finance

In the finance industry, AI contributes to:

Fraud Detection: AI systems detect fraudulent activities by analyzing transaction patterns and flagging unusual behaviors.

Algorithmic Trading: AI algorithms analyze market data and execute trades at high speeds, optimizing investment strategies.

Customer Service: Chatbots and virtual assistants provide customer support, handle inquiries, and manage transactions efficiently.

Transportation

AI is transforming transportation with advancements such as:

Autonomous Vehicles: Self-driving cars use AI to navigate roads, interpret traffic signals, and avoid obstacles, enhancing safety and efficiency.

Traffic Management: AI systems analyze traffic patterns to optimize traffic flow, reduce congestion, and manage public transportation systems.

Predictive Maintenance: AI predicts maintenance needs for vehicles and infrastructure, reducing downtime and improving reliability.

Retail

AI enhances the retail experience through:

Personalized Recommendations: AI algorithms analyze customer behavior to provide personalized product recommendations, increasing sales and customer satisfaction.

Inventory Management: AI predicts demand and manages inventory levels, optimizing supply chain operations.

Chatbots: AI-powered chatbots assist customers, answer queries, and facilitate online shopping experiences.

Manufacturing

In manufacturing, AI is utilized for:

Quality Control: AI systems inspect products for defects and ensure quality standards, reducing waste and improving efficiency.

Predictive Maintenance: AI monitors equipment performance and predicts failures, allowing proactive maintenance and reducing downtime.

Automation: AI automates repetitive tasks, such as assembly line work, enhancing productivity and precision.

Entertainment

AI contributes to the entertainment industry by:

Content Creation: AI generates music, art, and literature, opening new possibilities for creativity and innovation.

Recommendation Systems: AI suggests movies, music, and games based on user preferences, enhancing the user experience.

Virtual Reality (VR) and Augmented Reality (AR): AI improves VR and AR experiences by enhancing graphics, interactions, and immersion.

GENERATIVE AI

Generative AI is transforming the way we create. Now, humans guide while machines handle tasks that are dirty, dull, dangerous, or difficult. This shift allows us to focus on our core work—our ideas, vision, and purpose.

The Significance of Generative AI

Generative AI is a groundbreaking technology, comparable to the invention of photography and film. Just as photography allowed us to capture reality without needing an artist's interpretation, generative AI enables us to create art, music, and more without traditional skills. It provides quick access to information, generates text like news articles, blog post or product descriptions, and remember this is not an exhausted list.

This technology uses algorithms trained on existing data to produce music, speech, visual effects, and 3D assets. It acts as a 24/7 assistant, handling repetitive tasks and complex calculations, allowing us to focus on creativity and strategic thinking.

Generative AI has evolved from early neural networks in 2006 to the advanced models we see today, such ChatGPT.

The quality of AI-generated content has drastically improved, as shown by the leap in image quality from 2014 to 2022. Now, AI can produce coherent images and text from simple prompts.

Generative AI is transforming various professions and redefining our concept of work. It handles repetitive production tasks, freeing us to explore what makes us human, our curiosity, awareness, dreams, emotional intelligence, and vision. This new era allows us to focus on our unique human traits while AI assists with execution. The goal here is not to work against the machines, but to use it as a productivity tool. So, you may wonder what is in to you as a creative, or wannabe content creator. Well, that is what this book is dedicated for, so here are a few things AI can help you achieve in less time as a content creator.

1. Idea Generation

AI is revolutionizing the way content creators generate ideas by analyzing vast amounts of data from various sources. These sources include trending topics on social media, popular search queries, and historical content performance. By leveraging natural language processing (NLP) and machine learning algorithms, AI can identify emerging trends and suggest relevant and engaging topics. For example, a blogger might use AI to discover trending topics related to their niche, providing inspiration for new articles or social media posts. This capability allows creators to stay ahead of the curve and produce content that resonates with their audience's current interests and concerns.

2. Content Writing

AI-powered tools are now capable of writing entire articles, scripts, or even books. These tools utilize advanced NLP models that can generate coherent and contextually relevant text. AI can create drafts, product descriptions, and promotional content, often requiring minimal human intervention. For instance, platforms like GPT-4 can generate news articles, marketing copy, or creative writing pieces based on input prompts. This not only speeds up the writing process but also helps creators produce content at scale without sacrificing quality. By providing a strong initial draft, AI allows writers to focus on refining and personalizing the content rather than starting from scratch.

3. Image and Video Creation

AI extends its capabilities to the creation of visual content, including images and videos. AI tools can design graphics, edit videos, and even generate original visual content. For example, AI can create unique images based on text descriptions or analyze existing video footage to produce highlights and summaries. AI-driven design tools can assist in creating infographics, social media posts, or marketing visuals that are both eye-catching and informative. This technology not only enhances the aesthetic quality of content but also reduces the time and effort required to produce professional-grade visuals.

4. Editing and Proofreading

Editing and proofreading are critical components of the content creation process, and AI is significantly enhancing these tasks. AI-powered tools can automatically check for grammar, spelling, punctuation, and style issues, ensuring that the content is polished and professional. Tools like Grammarly or ProWritingAid provide real-time suggestions for improving clarity, coherence, and readability. Additionally, AI can ensure consistency in tone and style across different pieces of content, which is particularly useful for brands maintaining a cohesive voice. By handling these technical aspects, AI allows creators to focus more on the creative elements of their work.

5. Personalisation

AI excels at personalizing content to meet the preferences and behaviors of individual users. By analyzing user data, including browsing history, social media activity, and past interactions, AI can tailor content recommendations and messages to individual preferences. For instance, streaming services use AI to suggest movies or shows based on a user's viewing history, while e-commerce sites recommend products based on past purchases and browsing patterns. This level of personalization enhances user engagement and satisfaction, as content becomes more relevant and aligned with the user's interests.

6. SEO Optimization

Search engine optimization (SEO) is crucial for content visibility, and AI can significantly enhance this aspect. AI tools can analyze search engine algorithms and suggest keywords that are likely to improve a piece of content's ranking. They can also provide insights into the optimal length, structure, and readability of content. For example, tools like SurferSEO or Clearscope analyze top-performing content in a given niche and provide recommendations for optimizing new content. This helps creators produce SEO-friendly content that attracts more organic traffic and improves their visibility on search engines.

HOW AI HELPS CREATIVES

AI is a powerful ally for creatives, offering transformative benefits across various aspects of content creation. Primarily, AI saves valuable time by automating repetitive tasks such as editing, formatting, and initial content generation. By handling these mundane activities, creatives can redirect their focus towards more strategic and creative pursuits, fostering innovation and experimentation.

Moreover, AI enhances creativity by providing novel ideas and fresh perspectives. By analyzing vast amounts of data, AI can identify emerging trends and suggest unique content angles, helping creators break through creative blocks and explore new creative territories. This capability not only sparks inspiration but also empowers creatives to push boundaries and produce more original and compelling content.

AI also significantly increases productivity by streamlining workflows and optimizing processes. From content scheduling and distribution to performance analysis and audience engagement metrics, AI tools enable creators to manage and execute tasks more efficiently. This efficiency not only accelerates content production but also improves overall workflow management, allowing creatives to handle larger volumes of work without compromising quality.

Furthermore, AI contributes to improving content quality by ensuring accuracy, consistency, and adherence to best practices. AI-powered tools can proofread, edit, and optimize content for SEO, helping creators deliver polished and professional-grade materials. This automated quality control not only enhances the final output but also strengthens brand credibility and audience trust through consistently high-quality content.

Now let's break it down for you to understand this better.

1. Saves Time

One of the most significant benefits of AI for content creators is the automation of repetitive tasks. Tasks such as editing, formatting, and generating initial drafts can be time-consuming and often detract from the more creative aspects of content creation. AI tools streamline these processes, allowing creators to focus their time and energy on developing original ideas and refining their work. For instance, a content creator can use AI to quickly generate a draft of a blog post, which they can then refine and personalize, thus reducing the time required to produce high-quality content.

2. Enhances Creativity

AI not only saves time but also enhances creativity by providing fresh ideas and inspiration. AI tools can analyze existing content and suggest new angles or approaches, helping creators overcome writer's block and explore new creative directions. For example, an AI tool might analyze trending topics and suggest unique perspectives or related subtopics that the creator hadn't considered. This can spark new ideas and encourage experimentation, leading to more innovative and engaging content. By acting as a creative partner, AI helps creators push the boundaries of their work and develop more original and compelling content.

3. Increases Productivity

AI significantly boosts productivity by streamlining various aspects of the content creation process. From idea generation to content writing, editing, and optimization, AI tools can handle multiple tasks simultaneously, allowing creators to produce more content in less time. For instance, a social media manager can use AI to schedule posts, analyze performance metrics, and generate content ideas, all from a single platform. This integrated approach not only enhances efficiency but also allows creators to manage their workload more effectively, enabling them to focus on high-priority tasks and produce a higher volume of quality content.

4. Improves Quality

AI ensures high-quality output by catching errors, optimizing for SEO, and maintaining consistency in style and tone. For example, AI-powered editing tools can detect and correct grammatical errors, suggest stylistic improvements, and ensure that the content adheres to SEO best practices. This automated quality control helps maintain a high standard of content and reduces the risk of errors or inconsistencies that could detract from the overall effectiveness of the content. By enhancing the quality of the content, AI helps creators build trust and credibility with their audience.

5. Data Insights

AI provides valuable data insights that help content creators understand what works best for their audience. By analyzing metrics such as engagement rates, click-through rates, and audience demographics, AI tools can identify patterns and trends that inform content strategy. For example, AI can reveal which types of content are most popular among a particular audience segment, allowing creators to tailor their content accordingly. This data-driven approach helps creators make informed decisions and optimize their content to better meet the needs and preferences of their audience.

6. Personalized Experience

AI's ability to personalize content enhances the overall user experience by delivering content that is more relevant and engaging. By tailoring recommendations and messages to individual users, AI helps creators build stronger connections with their audience and increase engagement. For instance, a news website might use AI to personalize the articles displayed to each user based on their reading history and preferences. This personalized approach not only improves user satisfaction but also increases the likelihood of repeat visits and interactions, as users are more likely to engage with content that resonates with their interests and preferences.

AI is transforming content creation by providing tools that enhance every stage of the process, from idea generation and content writing to editing, personalization, and SEO optimization. These AI capabilities help content creators save time, boost productivity, enhance creativity, and improve the quality of their work. By leveraging AI, creators can focus more on strategic and inventive aspects of their projects, allowing them to produce more engaging, relevant, and high-quality content for their audiences. The integration of AI into content creation not only streamlines workflows but also opens up new possibilities for innovation and personalization, ultimately leading to a more effective and satisfying creative process.

Now, let's delve into the ethical and societal impact of AI.

THE ETHICAL AND SOCIETAL IMPACT OF AI

While AI offers tremendous benefits, it also raises ethical and societal concerns. As AI systems become more integrated into daily life, issues such as privacy, bias, and the future of work come to the forefront.

Privacy Concerns

AI systems often rely on vast amounts of data, including personal information. The collection, storage, and use of this data raise privacy concerns. For example, facial recognition systems can be used for surveillance, potentially infringing on individual privacy rights. Ensuring transparent data practices and consent mechanisms is crucial to address these concerns.

Bias and Fairness

AI systems can inherit biases from their training data, leading to unfair outcomes. For instance, if an AI system is trained on biased data, it may exhibit discriminatory behavior in hiring, lending, or law enforcement. Addressing bias in AI requires careful design, diverse data sources, and continuous monitoring to ensure fairness and equity.

CHAPTER 2
INTRODUCTION TO
CHATGPT

In this chapter, we delve into the fascinating world of ChatGPT, an advanced AI language model developed by OpenAI. ChatGPT represents a significant advancement in natural language processing technology, designed to understand and generate human-like text based on vast amounts of data it has been trained on.

ChatGPT stands as one of the most prominent examples of conversational AI, capable of generating human-like text based on the input it receives. It has applications ranging from customer service to creative writing. This chapter delves into what ChatGPT is, how it works, and its development, offering a solid foundation for understanding this advanced AI model.

WHAT IS CHATGPT?

ChatGPT, short for Chat Generative Pre-trained Transformers, is a sophisticated AI language model developed by OpenAI. It leverages the architecture of the Transformer, a deep learning model introduced by Vaswani et al. in 2017, to generate coherent and contextually relevant text.

KEY FEATURES OF CHATGPT

Conversational Ability: ChatGPT excels in understanding and generating human-like responses in natural language, making it ideal for chatbots, virtual assistants, and interactive applications.

Context Awareness: It can maintain context within a conversation, allowing it to provide relevant responses over multiple exchanges.

Versatility: ChatGPT can be used for a variety of tasks, including answering questions, writing essays, generating code, creating content, and more.

Language Support: It supports multiple languages, making it a versatile tool for global applications.

Next, I'll delve into how ChatGPT really works.

HOW CHATGPT WORKS

Understanding how ChatGPT works involves exploring its architecture, training process, and the mechanisms that enable it to generate text.

ChatGPT relies on a specific architecture called the Transformer. This architecture has several key components that work together to understand and generate language. One of these components is the attention mechanism. This mechanism allows the model to focus on the most important words in a sentence, regardless of their order. It does this by assigning weights to different words, similar to how humans pay more attention to certain words depending on the context.

Another key component is the use of layers. ChatGPT is built with multiple layers, each containing a combination of attention mechanisms and simpler neural networks. As the text data passes through these layers, its representation becomes more refined, allowing the model to capture increasingly complex relationships between words.

Finally, since Transformers don't inherently understand the order in which words appear, a technique called positional encoding is used. This encoding injects information about the order of words into the data, allowing the model to process the text as a sequence and understand the relationships between words based on their position in the sentence.

CHATGPT'S TRAINING PROCESS

ChatGPT's training can be broken down into two key steps. The first step is pre-training. During this phase, the model is exposed to a massive amount of text data collected from the internet. This data helps the model learn to predict the next word in a sequence, which allows it to grasp the nuances of grammar, factual information, and even develop some basic reasoning abilities. Throughout this process, the model's internal parameters are constantly adjusted to minimize the difference between its predictions and the actual text it's analyzing.

Once pre-training is complete, ChatGPT moves on to the fine-tuning stage. Here, the model is presented with a more targeted dataset. This data is often reviewed by human experts who provide feedback on the model's outputs. This feedback is crucial for incorporating safety measures and ensuring the model aligns its responses with human preferences and ethical guidelines.

Mechanism of Text Generation

ChatGPT creates text by taking educated guesses about the next word that should come in a sequence. Here's a simplified look at how it works:

First, it breaks down the text you give it into smaller pieces, like building blocks, that the system can understand. These pieces are called tokens.

Next, ChatGPT uses the clues from these tokens to figure out the probability of different words potentially coming next. Imagine a bunch of possible words, and each has a score based on how likely it is to fit.

The system then picks a word from this list of possibilities, considering the scores. This process continues, picking new words based on the previous ones, until it forms a complete response.

Finally, it translates those building blocks back into human language that you can read and understand. This method allows ChatGPT to craft responses that flow well and make sense in the context of the conversation, because it considers the back-and-forth as it generates text.

DEVELOPMENT AND VERSIONS OF CHATGPT

ChatGPT has evolved through several iterations, each improving upon its capabilities and addressing limitations of previous versions. Here's a brief overview of its development:

Early Models

GPT-1 (2018): The first iteration, GPT-1, introduced the concept of Generative Pre-trained Transformers. It demonstrated the potential of using transformers for language modeling but had limited conversational abilities.

GPT-2 (2019): GPT-2 was a significant improvement, featuring 1.5 billion parameters. It showed remarkable ability to generate coherent text, leading to concerns about misuse and initially limited its public release.

Advancements with GPT-3

GPT-3 (2020): GPT-3 brought a substantial leap forward with 175 billion parameters. It exhibited improved conversational abilities, understanding complex instructions, and generating more nuanced responses. This version of GPT-3 became widely known for its versatility in various applications.

Codex (2021): Derived from GPT-3, Codex was specifically fine-tuned for understanding and generating programming code, leading to applications like GitHub Copilot.

ChatGPT and Beyond

ChatGPT-3.5 (2021): Fine-tuned on conversational data, ChatGPT-3.5 improved contextual understanding and response coherence, making it more suitable for interactive applications.

ChatGPT-4 (2023): Introduced further enhancements in natural language understanding, conversational abilities, and multi-modal capabilities, allowing it to process images and text simultaneously. This iteration represents a significant advancement, expanding ChatGPT's capabilities to better interact and comprehend a wide array of user inputs across different modalities.

The latest version, ChatGPT at the time of writing this book is ChatGPT-4o. ChatGPT-4o was released in May 13, 2024. ChatGPT-4o represents the latest evolution in OpenAI's language model series. This version introduces substantial improvements in natural language processing, conversation handling, and multi-modal integration. ChatGPT-4o flagship model that can reason across audio, vision, and text in real time.

Its ability to understand and generate human-like text while also expanding its capacity to interpret and respond to combined text and image inputs, marking a significant stride forward in AI-driven communication and interaction capabilities.

KEY INNOVATIONS IN CHATGPT-4

ChatGPT-4 represents the latest advancements in AI language models. Key innovations include:

1. Improved Context Management: ChatGPT-4 can handle longer contexts and generate more relevant responses across extended conversations.

2. Enhanced Safety and Ethics: It incorporates more sophisticated mechanisms to avoid generating harmful or biased content, aligning with ethical guidelines more effectively.

3. Multi-Modal Capabilities: ChatGPT-4 can interpret and generate content based on both text and images, broadening its applicability to scenarios requiring visual understanding.

4. Personalization: It offers better personalization options, allowing users to fine-tune responses based on specific preferences and requirements.

APPLICATIONS OF CHATGPT

ChatGPT's versatile capabilities make it applicable across various domains. Here are some key applications:

Customer Support: ChatGPT powers chatbots and virtual assistants, providing immediate, accurate responses to customer queries. It can handle a wide range of customer service tasks, from answering FAQs to troubleshooting issues.

Content Creation: When it comes to content creation, ChatGPT assists in drafting articles, generating creative writing, and brainstorming ideas. It can be a valuable tool for writers, marketers, and educators, offering suggestions and completing drafts efficiently.

Education: ChatGPT acts as a tutor or teaching assistant, answering students' questions, providing explanations, and assisting with homework. It supports personalized learning by adapting to individual learning styles and needs.

Programming Assistance: ChatGPT helps programmers by generating code snippets, debugging, and offering suggestions for code optimization. Tools like GitHub Copilot, based on ChatGPT, enhance coding productivity and learning.

Entertainment: In entertainment, ChatGPT creates interactive narratives, writes dialogue for games, and even composes poetry or lyrics. It offers a novel way to engage with audiences and explore creative projects.

Healthcare: ChatGPT supports healthcare applications by providing medical information, assisting in diagnosis, and managing patient interactions. It can streamline administrative tasks and enhance patient engagement.

ETHICAL CONSIDERATIONS AND CHALLENGES

While ChatGPT offers a fascinating glimpse into the future of AI-powered communication, its immense potential comes hand-in-hand with significant ethical challenges that demand our attention. Here's a closer look at some of the key concerns:

1. Bias and Fairness

ChatGPT's training data is the foundation upon which it builds its understanding of the world. Unfortunately, the real world can be riddled with biases. If the data used to train ChatGPT isn't carefully curated to be diverse and representative, these biases can seep into the model's responses. Imagine asking ChatGPT for career advice, only to receive recommendations that favor certain professions based on unconscious biases within its training data. To address this, developers need to prioritize diverse training datasets and continuously monitor and refine ChatGPT's outputs to mitigate bias and ensure fairness.

2. Misinformation

ChatGPT's fluency in language can be a double-edged sword. It can craft highly believable text, even if the information it conveys is factually incorrect or misleading. This raises serious concerns, especially when it comes to sensitive topics like health or finance. Imagine receiving seemingly well-researched financial advice from ChatGPT, only to discover later that the information was inaccurate and led to costly mistakes. Equipping ChatGPT with robust fact-checking mechanisms and being transparent about its limitations are crucial steps in combating the spread of misinformation.

3. Privacy and Security

ChatGPT's capabilities raise questions about how it handles sensitive information. If we start using ChatGPT for tasks that involve personal data, robust safeguards need to be put in place. Following data protection regulations and ensuring users have clear control over their information are essential for responsible use of this technology. Imagine using ChatGPT to write a personal email, only to worry that the information might be leaked or misused. Trust and transparency are paramount when dealing with sensitive data.

4. Dependency and Misuse
As ChatGPT becomes more sophisticated, there's a risk of becoming overly reliant on its abilities. Tasks that require critical thinking, human judgment, and emotional intelligence should not be solely delegated to AI. Imagine relying solely on ChatGPT's analysis for a complex business decision, overlooking important nuances that a human might pick up on. Clear guidelines and human oversight are necessary to ensure ChatGPT remains a powerful tool that complements human decision-making, not replaces it.

By acknowledging these ethical challenges and implementing responsible development practices, we can harness the potential of ChatGPT while mitigating its potential pitfalls. This ensures AI advancements lead to a brighter future, not an ethically ambiguous one.

To conclude this chapter, ChatGPT represents a significant advancement in AI, offering powerful conversational abilities and broad applicability across various domains. From its underlying architecture and training process to its development through successive versions, ChatGPT has evolved into a sophisticated tool capable of enhancing human-machine interactions.

As we continue exploring the capabilities and applications of ChatGPT in subsequent chapters, understanding its foundation and development is crucial. This knowledge will inform the practical use of ChatGPT, enabling users to leverage its potential while navigating its challenges responsibly.

More on ethical consideration in chapter eight.

CHAPTER 3
GETTING STARTED WITH CHATGPT

ChatGPT offers a range of functionalities that can be harnessed for diverse applications, from generating creative content to providing customer support. This chapter will guide you through the initial steps of setting up and interacting with ChatGPT, helping you understand its basic operations and how to make the most of its capabilities.

Setting Up ChatGPT

To begin using ChatGPT, you must set up the necessary environment and understand the available platforms and interfaces.

Platforms and Access

ChatGPT is accessible through various platforms, including:

OpenAI Website: You can interact with ChatGPT directly on OpenAI's official website by signing up for an account and accessing their chat interface.

API Access: OpenAI offers an API that allows developers to integrate ChatGPT into applications. This requires setting up an API key and configuring the integration according to your needs.

Pre-built Applications: Many applications, such as coding assistants or customer service bots, use ChatGPT under the hood. These can be accessed directly through their respective platforms.

For the purpose of this book I will be using OpenAI website for creating an Account

To use ChatGPT via the OpenAI website, follow these steps: GO TO the [chatgpt.com/auth/login]

type this URL on your browser address

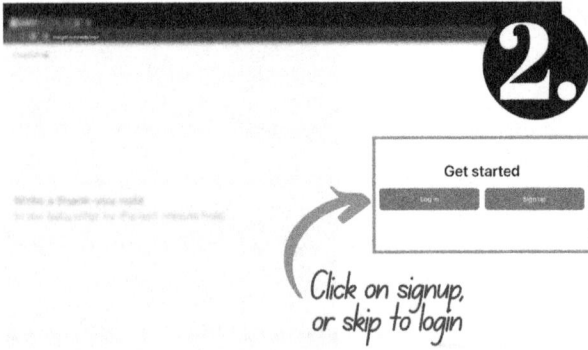

Get started

Click on signup, or skip to login

New user? Sign up! Existing user? Login!

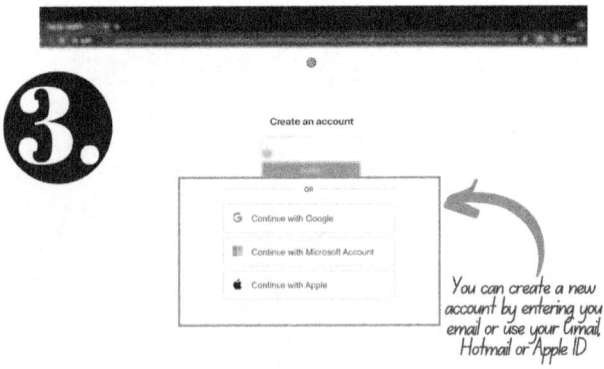

Create an account

or

G   Continue with Google

   Continue with Microsoft Account

  Continue with Apple

You can create a new account by entering you email or use your Gmail, Hotmail or Apple ID

I recommend you open a new gmail account and signup with Google Gmail, as it is seamless.

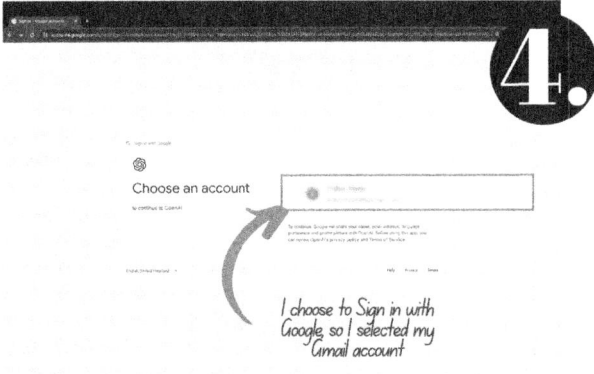

I choose to Sign in with Google, so I selected my Gmail account

All you have to do, is to choose the Gmail account to sign up with.

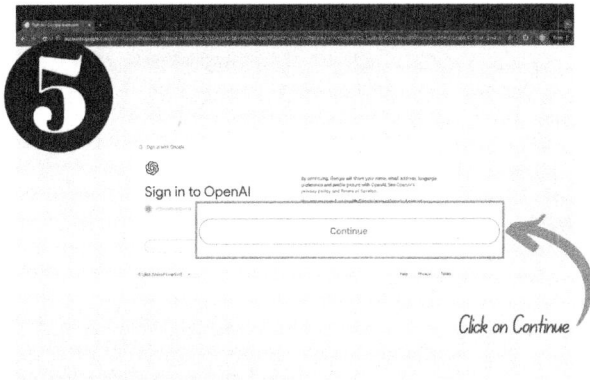

Click on Continue

Confirm your email address by following the verification link sent to your email.

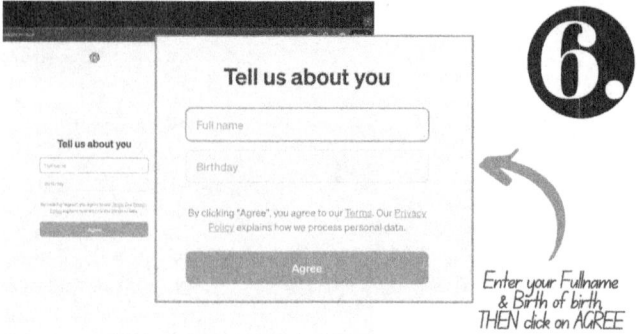

Tell us about you

Full name

Birthday

By clicking "Agree", you agree to our Terms. Our Privacy Policy explains how we process personal data.

Agree

Enter your Fullname & Birth of birth, THEN click on AGREE

Remember you must be 18 and above

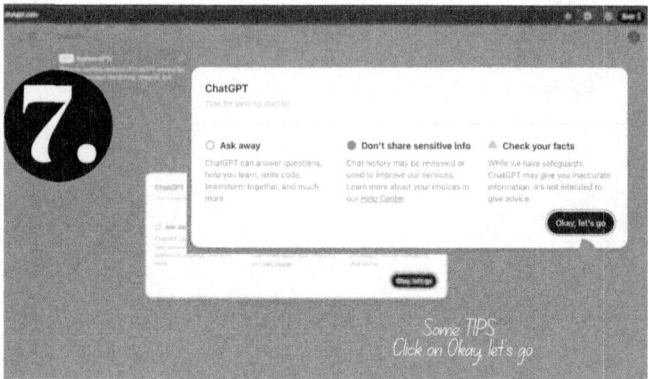

ChatGPT

○ Ask away

ChatGPT can answer questions, help you learn, write code, brainstorm together, and much more.

● Don't share sensitive info

Chat history may be reviewed or used to improve our services. Learn more about your choices in our Help Center.

✎ Check your facts

While we have safeguards, ChatGPT may give you inaccurate information. It's not intended to give advice.

Okay, let's go

Some TIPS Click on Okay, let's go

When you get to this phase, you are all set.

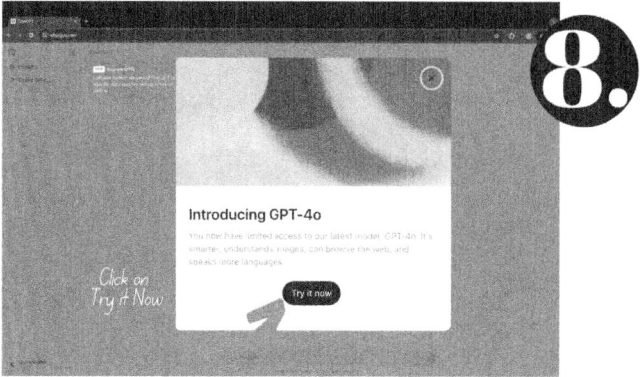

8.

Click on Try it Now

Introducing GPT-4o

You now have unified access to our latest model, GPT-4o. It is smarter, understands images, can browse the web, and speaks more languages.

Try it now

This book references ChatGPT as using GPT-4o, the most advanced version available at the time of writing.

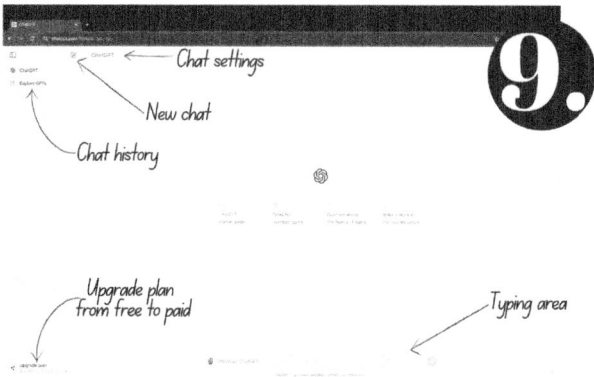

9.

Chat settings

New chat

Chat history

Upgrade plan from free to paid

Typing area

ChatGPT workspace

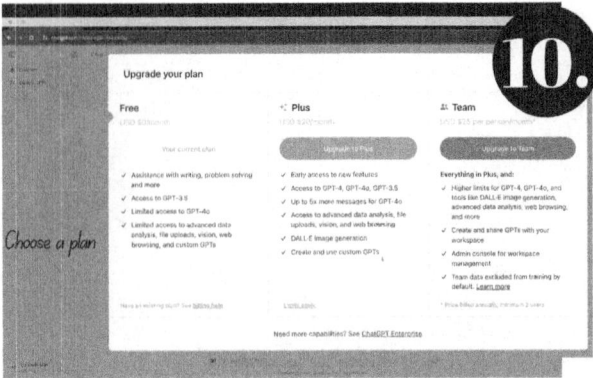

10.

Choose a plan

Upgrade your plan

Free	Plus	Team

Choose a Plan: OpenAI offers various subscription plans, including a free tier with limited usage and paid tiers with more features and higher usage limits.

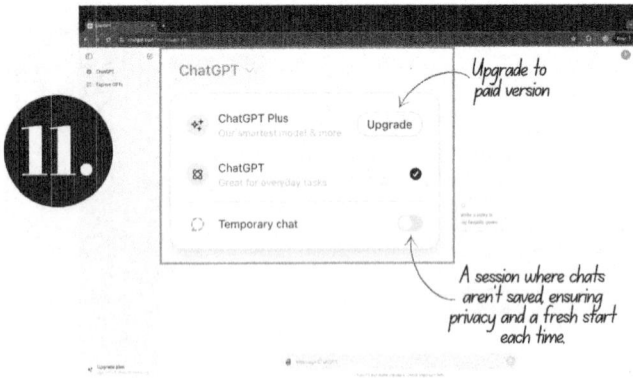

11.

ChatGPT ∨

Upgrade to paid version

✦ ChatGPT Plus — Upgrade

▨ ChatGPT ✓

○ Temporary chat

A session where chats aren't saved, ensuring privacy and a fresh start each time.

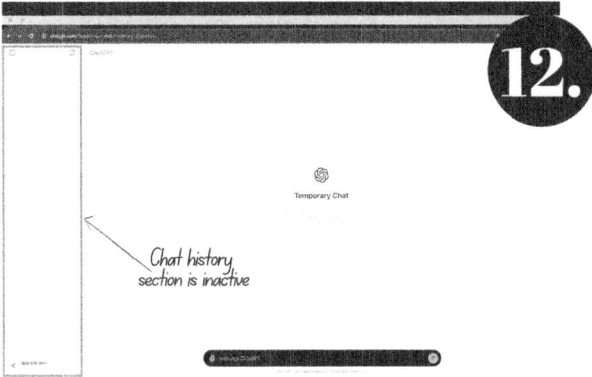

12.

Chat history section is inactive

Temporary Chat

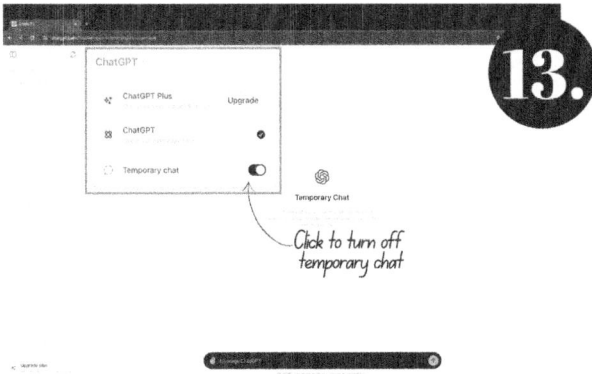

13.

ChatGPT

ChatGPT Plus   Upgrade

ChatGPT

Temporary chat

Temporary Chat

Click to turn off temporary chat

These are the steps you need to setup your account with OpenAI and start using ChatGPT.

The ChatGPT workspace includes:

Your Prompt: The section where users input their questions or commands.

ChatGPT Response: The area where the AI generates and displays its answers or outputs based on the prompt.

Typing Area: A text box where users type their queries or instructions to interact with ChatGPT.

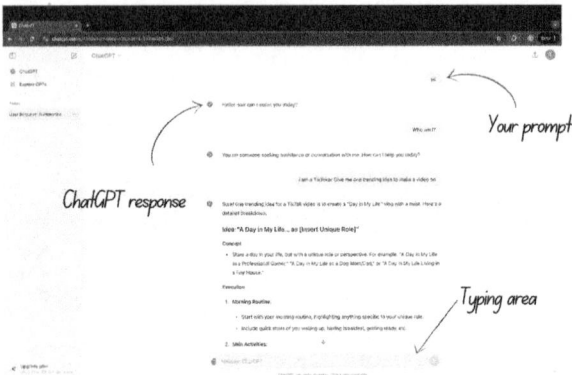

SETTING UP THE API

If you plan to integrate ChatGPT into your applications via the API:

1. Generate an API Key: Once logged in to your OpenAI account, navigate to the API section and generate a new API key.

2. Install API Client: Install the OpenAI Python client or any other preferred language client to interact with the API.

INTERACTING WITH CHATGPT

Once ChatGPT is set up, you can start interacting with it. Understanding how to craft inputs and interpret outputs is essential for effective use.

Crafting Effective Prompts

The prompt is the input text you provide to ChatGPT, guiding it to generate relevant responses. Here's how to craft effective prompts:

1. Be Clear and Specific: Ensure your prompt clearly states what you want. Ambiguous prompts may lead to vague or unrelated responses.
   Example: Instead of "Tell me about dogs," use "Describe the characteristics and care requirements of Golden Retrievers."

2. Provide Context: Include enough context in your prompt to guide the response.

Example: "I'm planning a trip to Paris. What are some must-see attractions for a first-time visitor?"

3. Use Examples: For more complex queries, providing examples can help guide ChatGPT.
Example: "Can you write a brief introduction to a research paper on climate change? Here's a sample introduction to another paper for reference."

4. Set Expectations: If you need a response in a specific format or style, mention it in your prompt.
Example: "Generate a professional email requesting a meeting with a potential client."

EXPLORING CAPABILITIES

Experiment with different types of queries to understand the range of ChatGPT's capabilities:

General Information: Ask factual questions or request summaries on various topics.
Example: "What are the primary causes of the French Revolution?"

Creative Writing: Request ChatGPT to generate stories, poems, or dialogues.
Example: "Write a short story about a detective solving a mystery in a small town."

Code Assistance: Use ChatGPT for programming help, such as code snippets or debugging.
Example: "How do I write a Python function to calculate the factorial of a number?"

Language Translation: Ask ChatGPT to translate text between languages.
Example: "Translate the following English sentence to Spanish: 'Where is the nearest restaurant?'"

Understanding Responses

Interpreting ChatGPT's responses effectively involves recognizing its strengths and limitations. ChatGPT's responses are based on patterns it has learned from its training data. Evaluate the response quality by considering:

Relevance: Does the response address your prompt accurately? If not, consider refining your prompt for clarity.
Coherence: Is the response logically structured and easy to understand?
Creativity: For creative tasks, does the response exhibit originality and creativity?

Handling Uncertainty

ChatGPT may sometimes generate uncertain or incorrect responses. Here's how to handle such scenarios:

Verification: For factual queries, cross-check the response with reliable sources to ensure accuracy.
Clarification: If the response is unclear, ask follow-up questions to refine the information.
Iterative Refinement: Adjust your prompt and try again if the initial response doesn't meet your expectations.

USING RESPONSE CONTROL MECHANISMS

OpenAI's ChatGPT stands out not only for its impressive ability to generate human-like text but also for the nuanced control it offers over its responses. Central to this control are the parameters provided by OpenAI, which allow users to tailor the behavior and output of ChatGPT to better suit their needs and preferences.

One of the key parameters offered by OpenAI is 'Max Tokens'. This parameter plays a crucial role in determining the length of ChatGPT's responses. Essentially, max tokens restricts the number of tokens, or words and symbols, that ChatGPT can output in its response. By setting a maximum limit, users can ensure that responses remain concise and focused on the essential information. This feature is particularly useful in scenarios where brevity is paramount, such as in chat interfaces, social media posts, or automated customer service responses.

For instance, in customer support applications, limiting the max tokens helps ChatGPT provide succinct and clear answers to user inquiries without overwhelming them with unnecessary details. Similarly, in educational settings, this parameter can aid in generating concise explanations or summaries of complex concepts, making learning materials more digestible and accessible to students.

Beyond controlling the length of responses, OpenAI provides additional parameters that influence the quality and style of ChatGPT's output. These parameters include options to adjust the temperature, which affects the creativity and variability of responses, and the presence of offensive language filters to ensure appropriateness in different contexts.

The 'Temperature' parameter, for example, regulates the randomness of ChatGPT's responses. A lower temperature value results in more predictable and safe responses, adhering closely to the training data and generating more conventional answers. Conversely, increasing the temperature introduces more diversity and creativity in responses, allowing ChatGPT to generate more imaginative or unexpected outputs. This flexibility is particularly valuable in creative writing, brainstorming sessions, or scenarios where exploring alternative perspectives is beneficial.

Moreover, OpenAI incorporates a 'Response Length' parameter, which enables users to specify the desired length of responses in terms of characters. This feature is beneficial when integrating ChatGPT into applications with strict character limits, such as social media platforms or messaging interfaces. By setting an appropriate response length, developers and users can ensure that ChatGPT's output aligns with the platform's constraints while maintaining clarity and relevance.

These control mechanisms not only empower users to customize ChatGPT's behavior but also enhance its applicability across diverse use cases. For businesses integrating AI into customer interactions, these parameters enable the creation of tailored chatbots that deliver consistent, on-brand responses. In educational environments, educators can leverage these controls to foster interactive learning experiences that adapt to individual student needs, providing personalized feedback and explanations.

How to use Max Tokens, Response Length and Temperature

Certainly! Here are detailed sample prompts for each of the parameters—Max Tokens, Response Length, and Temperature—used with ChatGPT:

1. Max Tokens

Prompt: "Could you limit the response to 50 tokens?"

Explanation: This prompt instructs ChatGPT to generate a response that contains a maximum of 50 tokens (words or subwords). This helps in keeping the response concise and to the point, which is useful in scenarios where brevity is important, such as in summaries or quick answers.

Example Interaction
User: "Could you limit the response to 50 tokens?"
ChatGPT: "Sure! I'll keep it brief. Here's the summary: [response within 50 tokens]."

2. Response Length

Prompt: "Please keep the response under 300 characters."

Explanation: This prompt specifies that the response generated by ChatGPT should not exceed 300 characters in length. It ensures that the response remains concise and fits within a specific character limit, which is useful for contexts such as social media posts, SMS messages, or other platforms with character restrictions.

Example Interaction
User: "Please keep the response under 300 characters."
ChatGPT: "Got it! Here's a concise answer: [response within 300 characters]."

3. Temperature:

Prompt: "Increase the temperature to 0.9 for more creative responses."

Explanation: This prompt adjusts the "temperature" parameter in ChatGPT, which controls the randomness of responses. A higher temperature (closer to 1.0) allows for more creative and diverse responses, sometimes introducing more imaginative or unexpected outputs. This can be useful in brainstorming sessions, creative writing prompts, or when exploring alternative perspectives.

Example Interaction
User: "Increase the temperature to 0.9 for more creative responses."
ChatGPT: "Sure! Let's get creative: [response with increased randomness and creativity]."

These prompts illustrate how you can effectively communicate your preferences to ChatGPT regarding response length, maximum tokens, and the level of creativity or randomness in generated responses. Adjusting these parameters can help tailor the interaction to better suit different contexts and communication styles.

CHAPTER 4
UNDERSTANDING
THE USER

Crafting Effective Prompts through Data Points

Crafting effective prompts is an art that begins with understanding the user on a fundamental level. This process is not merely about generating grammatically correct responses but about delivering answers that are relevant, personalized, and meaningful to the user's context. In the era of data-driven solutions, one cannot underestimate the value of knowing the user, their preferences, and their behavior. A thoughtful analysis of the user can significantly elevate the quality of AI interactions, ensuring that responses resonate with the intended audience. This chapter delves into how data points related to user behavior, preferences, and past interactions can be leveraged to refine AI-generated prompts, ultimately creating more engaging, accurate, and relevant interactions.

THE IMPORTANCE OF USER UNDERSTANDING IN PROMPT CRAFTING

When it comes to crafting prompts, understanding the user enables the creation of interactions that are highly personalized. This personalization results in numerous benefits for AI systems, enhancing user satisfaction and fostering better engagement. The primary ways in which understanding the user influences prompt outcomes can be categorized as relevance, engagement, and accuracy.

1. Relevance

The effectiveness of an AI prompt is often judged by how relevant its response is to the user's question or task. When the AI has insights into the user's needs, preferences, or goals, it can generate prompts that are more contextually appropriate. For example, a user frequently asking for financial advice might benefit from prompts that include more specialized terms or suggestions tailored to their financial background. By employing user data—such as previous interactions, known preferences, or demographic information—AI systems can provide answers that speak directly to the user's unique situation, increasing the utility of the interaction. This ensures that the response doesn't feel generic or out of touch with the user's specific needs.

2. Engagement

Engagement is a critical factor in AI interactions, especially for systems designed to maintain long-term user relationships. Users are more likely to engage with AI systems that understand their individual preferences and exhibit a human-like ability to remember and incorporate past conversations into current interactions. By leveraging user data points, AI can create prompts that not only align with the user's interests but also anticipate their next logical query. For instance, an AI could offer follow-up questions or suggestions based on the user's past inquiries, encouraging deeper exploration of the topic. This fosters a sense of dialogue, as the system seems to "understand" the user, creating more dynamic and satisfying exchanges.

3. Accuracy

While relevance and engagement are vital, accuracy is perhaps the most essential factor for effective AI interactions. If the AI provides inaccurate or irrelevant information, user trust can be quickly eroded. Understanding the user through data points helps the AI fine-tune its responses, filtering out unnecessary or irrelevant details. This is particularly important when dealing with complex or sensitive subjects, such as health advice or legal information, where even slight inaccuracies can have serious consequences. By knowing who the user is—such as their expertise level or specific needs—the AI can adjust its tone, complexity, and focus, ensuring that the response is not only correct but appropriate for the user's knowledge base.

Data-Driven User Insights: The Foundation of Effective Prompts

To achieve a deep understanding of the user, data-driven insights play a pivotal role. Data points such as user demographics, behavioral patterns, and interaction histories provide the foundation for crafting personalized prompts. By analyzing these data points, AI systems can move beyond one-size-fits-all responses to more bespoke interactions. These insights allow the system to:

Predict user intent: By understanding previous behaviors and preferences, AI can predict what the user might ask next, enabling more proactive prompts.

Segment user types: Grouping users by characteristics (such as novice vs. expert) allows the system to adjust prompts based on the level of detail or sophistication required.

Optimize tone and style: Different users respond to different communication styles, and understanding user preferences can guide the AI to adopt the most effective tone—be it formal, casual, technical, or conversational.

PERSONA: DEFINING WHO THE USER IS

A user persona is a composite profile that represents a segment of the intended audience, developed through a deep understanding of their demographic, psychographic, and behavioral characteristics. In the context of AI interactions, particularly when crafting effective prompts, creating a persona helps ensure that the system caters to the user's needs, preferences, and behaviors. By simulating real users, personas guide the creation of more personalized and engaging interactions, which leads to a more satisfying and user-centric experience.

Personas go beyond surface-level characteristics. They encapsulate the user's deeper motivations, preferences, and interaction styles. For instance, a persona may reflect a user's comfort with technology, their expectations for communication, and their personal or professional goals. Understanding who the user is at a granular level makes it easier to tailor content and responses that resonate, thus enhancing engagement and overall user satisfaction.

Behavioral Traits

Behavioral traits refer to how users typically interact with a product, service, or system. These traits are critical in shaping user interactions because they reveal preferred communication styles, the depth of detail they seek, and their interaction habits.

For example, consider users who are highly tech-savvy and comfortable with digital tools. These users are likely to prefer more concise, efficient communication. They may expect quick responses that get straight to the point and skip over any unnecessary details. On the other hand, users who are less familiar with technology or need more hand-holding may appreciate a more guided and detailed explanation.

Behavioral traits might also include a user's tolerance for ambiguity. Some users may seek definitive, clear-cut answers, while others may appreciate nuanced responses that explore different possibilities. Crafting prompts that align with these preferences ensures a smoother, more intuitive interaction. In addition, behavioral insights can highlight whether users prefer textual, visual, or multimedia information. A persona built on these traits creates a strong foundation for designing prompts that meet the user where they are, optimizing their experience.

Interests and Motivations

Understanding a user's interests, hobbies, and motivations provides valuable context for designing interactions that feel relevant and engaging. Interests can reveal the topics a user is likely to engage with, while motivations uncover the underlying reasons for their behavior. Whether someone is driven by curiosity, a desire for efficiency, or the need to connect socially, these factors guide how prompts should be framed.

For example, a persona for a college student may emphasize the need for quick, fact-based information to help them with assignments. Their interest may revolve around academic topics, and their motivation may be task-oriented, pushing them to seek concise and accurate answers. In contrast, a hobbyist researching a niche topic like vintage cars may appreciate long, exploratory discussions that dive deep into their area of interest. Their motivation stems from passion and personal fulfillment, so prompts that encourage detailed exploration will resonate more.

Understanding these elements also allows for emotional connections to be built. Motivational triggers such as career advancement, personal growth, or mastery of a skill can be integrated into the AI's responses. For instance, a working professional seeking career advice might respond positively to prompts that not only provide guidance but also offer motivational elements and reflective insights. A prompt like, "What skills would help you achieve your career goals this year?" adds an element of reflection, encouraging deeper engagement.

Examples of Personas

- A college student persona could reflect someone seeking fast, factual answers to support their learning process. Their responses should be concise, actionable, and fact-driven, focusing on delivering the necessary information efficiently.

- A working professional persona, particularly someone seeking career advice, may benefit from prompts that are more nuanced and thoughtful. This persona values personal and professional growth, so prompts could focus on self-reflection, goal-setting, and professional development strategies.

- A hobbyist persona, such as someone interested in a niche subject like astronomy or history, would likely appreciate deeper, exploratory discussions. Prompts for this user should encourage curiosity and offer detailed information to satisfy their passion for the topic.

In sum, creating a persona ensures that interactions are user-centered, fostering more personalized and meaningful experiences. By deeply understanding the user's behavioral traits, interests, and motivations, personas enable the crafting of prompts that meet the user's specific needs and preferences, leading to a higher level of engagement and satisfaction.

KNOWING THE USER: GATHERING RELEVANT INFORMATION

To create a meaningful and personalized user experience, it is essential to understand the user's expectations, needs, and preferences. This process begins with gathering relevant data, which can be achieved through two main methods: direct communication and implicit cues. These approaches help refine interactions, allowing for more targeted and effective responses.

Direct User Communication

Direct communication is the most straightforward way to gather information about the user's needs. It involves asking clear and specific questions that guide the user to articulate their expectations. This method can be particularly useful in clarifying ambiguous situations where the user's intentions may not be immediately obvious. For instance, open-ended questions like, "What are you hoping to achieve?" or "How can I assist you today?" encourage the user to provide detailed responses. These questions allow the user to explain their goals and give insight into the type of help they need.

In addition to open-ended inquiries, follow-up questions can further narrow down specific details. For example, after a user mentions they need help with a project, asking, "Could you elaborate on the challenges you're facing with this project?" would help focus on areas that require attention. This kind of dialogue allows for a deeper understanding of the problem and enhances the precision of the assistance offered.

Clear communication also fosters a sense of involvement for the user, showing that their input is valued. When users feel heard and understood, they are more likely to engage openly, share relevant information, and trust the interaction. The interaction becomes a collaborative process, with both the user and the system working together to find the best solution.

Implicit User Cues

While direct communication is important, users may not always fully articulate their needs, or they may offer subtle hints that can guide the conversation. This is where implicit user cues come into play. Implicit cues are pieces of information that can be inferred from the user's behavior, tone, language choices, and prior interactions.

For instance, the formality or informality of a user's language can be a strong indicator of their communication style. A user who uses casual phrases and emojis may prefer a more relaxed, conversational tone in the responses. On the other hand, a user who speaks in formal, technical terms might expect a more professional and precise tone. Adjusting communication style based on these subtle signals can improve rapport and make the interaction feel more natural to the user.

Additionally, implicit cues can reveal emotional states or levels of urgency. A user repeatedly mentioning time constraints or using words like "urgent" or "ASAP" signals the need for quicker responses. Conversely, a user expressing frustration through words like "confused" or "stuck" might benefit from more empathetic and reassuring guidance. Recognizing these cues allows for adjustments not only in tone but also in the content of the responses, tailoring them to better match the user's emotional and situational context.

Active listening in the context of AI goes beyond just processing words; it involves understanding the nuances behind the user's statements. Capturing these subtleties allows for more proactive assistance. For instance, if a user has a history of similar queries, anticipating their next steps or concerns can speed up the resolution process and enhance the overall experience.

So, knowing the user requires a balanced approach that combines both direct communication and the interpretation of implicit cues. By engaging in meaningful dialogue and paying attention to the user's subtle signals, interactions become more relevant, personalized, and efficient.

DEMOGRAPHIC DATA POINTS: WHAT YOU NEED TO KNOW

Understanding demographic data is essential for tailoring communication strategies effectively. This data provides a foundational grasp of the user's identity, which is crucial in crafting prompts that resonate. By dissecting the various demographic factors, organizations can fine-tune their messaging to meet the expectations and preferences of different user segments. Here's an in-depth look at how age, gender, location, and socioeconomic status influence communication strategies:

Age

Age is a significant determinant in shaping communication style. Younger users often engage more with casual, conversational language peppered with contemporary slang and cultural references. This demographic is typically accustomed to rapid, informal exchanges and is more likely to appreciate a tone that mirrors social media interactions or trending topics. For instance, a marketing prompt targeting millennials might use emojis, pop culture references, or informal language to connect effectively.

Conversely, older users may respond better to a more formal and respectful tone. This group might value clarity, professionalism, and a structured approach. In this case, the language should be less informal, focusing on straightforward information and a respectful tone. Tailoring the content to reflect these preferences helps in building trust and ensuring the message is well-received.

Gender

Gender can influence communication preferences, though it's essential to approach this factor sensitively and avoid reinforcing stereotypes. Men and women may have different styles of engagement based on societal norms and personal preferences. For example, research suggests that women often prefer detailed explanations and collaborative language, while men might appreciate direct and action-oriented prompts. However, these preferences are not universal and can vary significantly within any gender group.

A nuanced understanding of gender differences can guide how to frame prompts. For instance, when creating content for a health and wellness application, recognizing that female users might prefer prompts that emphasize holistic well-being

57

and community support could improve engagement. Meanwhile, male users might respond better to prompts that highlight efficiency and goal-setting.

Location

Geographic location influences communication in several ways, including cultural nuances, language variations, and regional customs. A user's location can determine the appropriateness of certain idiomatic expressions, slang, or cultural references. For example, a marketing campaign for a product in the United States might incorporate American idioms and cultural references that resonate locally but may be confusing or irrelevant to users in other countries.

Additionally, location can impact the formality of language. In some cultures, formal communication is the norm, while in others, a more relaxed style is preferred. By tailoring prompts to reflect local customs and language preferences, organizations can enhance the relevance and relatability of their messages.

Socioeconomic Status

Socioeconomic status plays a crucial role in shaping communication strategies. Users from different economic backgrounds may have distinct priorities, expectations, and concerns. For example, individuals from lower socioeconomic backgrounds might be more focused on budgeting and cost-saving tips, while those from higher socioeconomic backgrounds may be more interested in investment strategies or luxury products.

Understanding these differences allows for the creation of prompts that address the specific needs and aspirations of each socioeconomic group. For instance, a financial advice service could design budgeting tips for users from lower-income brackets and sophisticated investment advice for those in higher income brackets. This approach not only meets the users' immediate needs but also respects their financial realities.

Case Study

Consider a financial advice service aiming to improve its engagement through personalized prompts. By analyzing user demographics, the service discovered that younger users from lower socioeconomic backgrounds were more interested in practical budgeting tips and debt management strategies. In contrast, older users with higher incomes preferred in-depth investment advice and retirement planning insights. By aligning the prompts with these preferences—providing budgeting tools and financial literacy content for younger users, and advanced investment strategies for older users—the service significantly enhanced its relevance and user satisfaction.

So, demographic data provides a crucial lens through which to view and tailor communication strategies. By understanding and applying insights related to age, gender, location, and socioeconomic status, organizations can craft prompts that are not only relevant but also engaging and respectful of the diverse needs of their audience.

Psychographic data offers a profound look into the inner workings of users beyond mere demographics. While demographic data—such as age, gender, and location—provides a foundational understanding of who users are, psychographic data delves deeper into their internal worlds. This type of data explores users' beliefs, values, lifestyles, and emotional triggers, offering a more nuanced perspective that can significantly enhance the relevance and resonance of interactions.

User Attitudes and Values

One of the core aspects of psychographic data is understanding user attitudes and values. These elements are crucial in shaping how users respond to various prompts and content. For instance, a user who places a high value on environmental sustainability is likely to appreciate content and interactions that reflect this value. This could mean preferring conversations that focus on eco-friendly practices or supporting green initiatives. Conversely, a user with a strong belief in technological advancement might engage more positively with content highlighting the latest innovations or futuristic trends. By tailoring responses to align with these attitudes and values, AI can craft interactions that feel more personal and relevant, enhancing user satisfaction and engagement.

User Interests and Hobbies

Another critical dimension of psychographic data is users' interests and hobbies. Recognizing and incorporating these interests into interactions can significantly boost engagement. For example, if an AI system knows that a user is passionate about gardening, it can provide gardening tips, suggest related content, or discuss recent trends in horticulture. This personalized approach not only makes interactions more engaging but also helps in building a deeper connection between the AI and the user. By aligning prompts with users' hobbies, the AI can make conversations more meaningful and enjoyable, thereby increasing the likelihood of positive user experiences and ongoing interaction.

Emotional Triggers

Understanding a user's emotional triggers is another vital aspect of psychographic data. Emotional triggers are specific stimuli that elicit a strong emotional response. For instance, a user who is particularly sensitive to stress might appreciate an AI response that is calming and reassuring when they express frustration. Conversely, an enthusiastic user might respond better to energetic and upbeat interactions. By recognizing these emotional cues, the AI can adjust its tone and style to better suit the user's current emotional state. This empathetic approach can enhance the overall user experience, making interactions feel more supportive and tailored to individual needs.

Incorporating psychographic data into AI interactions enables a more personalized and empathetic approach to communication. By understanding and responding to users' attitudes, values, interests, and emotional states, AI can create a more engaging and resonant experience. This deeper level of interaction goes beyond surface-level engagement, fostering stronger connections and a greater sense of understanding between users and AI systems. In essence, leveraging psychographic data allows for more thoughtful, contextually relevant, and emotionally attuned interactions, making AI not just a tool but a more integrated and responsive participant in users' digital lives.

UNDERSTANDING THE DIFFERENCE: DEMOGRAPHICS VS. PSYCHOGRAPHICS

In the realm of user experience and personalized communication, understanding the distinction between demographics and psychographics is crucial. While both types of data are integral to developing a nuanced understanding of users, they serve different functions and offer unique insights. Recognizing how to effectively leverage both can significantly enhance the effectiveness of prompts and interactions, leading to a more personalized and engaging user experience.

Demographics: Defining "Who"

Demographic data encompasses the quantifiable attributes of individuals, answering questions related to their identity and background. This includes fundamental characteristics such as age, gender, location, education level, and occupation. For instance, knowing that a user is a 30-year-old male living in New York with a background in finance provides a broad-stroke overview of their identity. This information is invaluable for segmenting users into meaningful groups and tailoring general content or services to fit specific demographic profiles.

Demographics are particularly useful for crafting messages that are contextually relevant and appropriate for various segments. For example, marketing campaigns often use demographic data to target specific age groups or genders with products and services designed to appeal to their life stage or gender-specific preferences. However, while demographic data can tell us "who" the user is, it often falls short in explaining "why" they behave the way they do.

Psychographics: Defining "Why"

Psychographic data delves deeper into the psychological attributes of users, providing insights into their values, interests, lifestyles, and motivations. This type of data answers questions about why users think and act the way they do. It explores their attitudes, beliefs, and aspirations, offering a more profound understanding of their emotional and psychological drivers.

For example, psychographic information might reveal that a user is passionate about sustainability, values work-life balance, and seeks out experiences that align with these principles. This knowledge allows for the crafting of messages and prompts that resonate on a deeper emotional level, addressing the user's intrinsic motivations and aligning with their personal values.

PRACTICAL APPLICATION: BLENDING DEMOGRAPHICS AND PSYCHOGRAPHICS

The most impactful communication strategies harness the strengths of both demographic and psychographic data. By combining these insights, you can create prompts that are not only factually accurate but also emotionally compelling. This holistic approach allows for a richer, more nuanced understanding of users, leading to interactions that feel both relevant and personally engaging.

Consider a scenario where you are developing personalized career advice. If you know a user's age and professional background (demographic data), you can provide advice that is contextually appropriate for their career stage. For example, a 30-year-old with a finance background might receive guidance focused on advancing within their field or transitioning to management roles.

By integrating psychographic data, such as the user's preference for risk-taking or desire for meaningful work, you can further refine this advice. A user who is risk-averse might receive career strategies that emphasize stability and incremental progress, while someone with a high risk tolerance might be encouraged to pursue entrepreneurial ventures or unconventional career paths. This blend of demographic and psychographic data ensures that the advice is not only practical but also aligns with the user's personal aspirations and values.

So, understanding and utilizing both demographic and psychographic data is essential for crafting prompts and messages that resonate with users on multiple levels. Demographics provide a foundational understanding of "who" users are, while psychographics offer insight into "why" they think and behave the way they do. When these elements are combined, they enable the creation of more targeted, effective, and emotionally engaging interactions, ultimately leading to a more personalized and satisfying user experience.

Examples and Case Studies: Crafting Tailored Prompts

In the realm of personalized communication and marketing, crafting tailored prompts that resonate with specific audience segments can significantly enhance engagement and effectiveness. By leveraging both demographic and psychographic data, organizations can create more relevant and compelling messages. Here's a deeper dive into how these data types can be utilized, illustrated with practical examples and a case study.

Using Demographic Data

Demographic data such as age, gender, income, and educational background provides a foundational understanding of a target audience's basic characteristics. This information is crucial for tailoring messages that align with the audience's stage in life or professional development. For instance, consider a career advice platform aiming to assist young adults and seasoned professionals. A 25-year-old recent graduate might seek concise, actionable career tips that address immediate job search challenges or networking strategies. This age group is likely to appreciate brief, motivational prompts that offer quick wins and practical advice on entering the job market.

Conversely, a 45-year-old professional, with years of experience and a more developed career path, might benefit from a reflective, strategic approach. This demographic may be interested in long-term career growth, leadership development, or transitioning to new roles. Tailoring prompts to offer in-depth analyses, strategic insights, and comprehensive planning tools will cater to their more mature career stage, helping them navigate complex career decisions or advancements.

Using Psychographic Data

Psychographic data dives deeper into an individual's interests, values, and lifestyle choices. This type of data is essential for crafting messages that resonate on a personal level. For example, an environmentally conscious traveler would likely appreciate travel tips that focus on sustainable practices, such as eco-friendly accommodations, green transportation options, or minimizing carbon footprints. Such prompts align with their values and enhance the relevance of the advice provided.

On the other hand, a more pragmatic user who prioritizes cost over environmental impact might respond better to tips highlighting budget-friendly travel options, discounts, and deals. Understanding these psychographic preferences ensures that the advice not only fits the user's values but also aligns with their practical needs.

Combining Both Data Types

Integrating both demographic and psychographic data creates a comprehensive profile of the target audience, allowing for highly customized prompts. For example, consider a health-conscious, middle-aged user living in a metropolitan area. This user's demographic data indicates they are likely balancing a busy urban lifestyle, while their psychographic data reveals a strong commitment to health and wellness.

A fitness app targeting this user might offer tailored prompts that emphasize quick, convenient workouts that can easily fit into a busy schedule. Tips could include exercises that can be done at home or in small spaces, recommendations for time-efficient routines, and guidance on maintaining a healthy lifestyle despite a hectic urban environment. By addressing both their demographic context and psychographic motivations, the app ensures that the fitness advice is not only practical but also aligned with their wellness goals.

Case Study

A notable example of tailoring prompts effectively is seen in the fitness app "FitLife." This app uses a sophisticated algorithm to analyze users' age, income, and fitness motivations, resulting in highly personalized workout recommendations. For younger users, FitLife focuses on quick, high-energy workouts that cater to their need for instant gratification and fitness results. These workouts are designed to be engaging and intense, aligning with the lifestyle and preferences of a younger demographic.

In contrast, older users receive prompts for balanced, low-impact routines that emphasize overall wellness and joint health. The app offers routines that are gentle on the body, suitable for users who may be more concerned about injury prevention and long-term health. These tailored recommendations reflect both the demographic data (such as age) and psychographic data (such as a focus on wellness), resulting in higher user satisfaction and engagement.

So, crafting tailored prompts by integrating demographic and psychographic data ensures that communication is both relevant and impactful. By addressing users' specific characteristics and preferences, organizations can significantly enhance the effectiveness of their messaging and foster a deeper connection with their audience.

SUMMARY: THE POWER OF USER UNDERSTANDING IN AI INTERACTIONS

In the evolving landscape of artificial intelligence (AI), the effectiveness of AI interactions hinges significantly on the depth of understanding we have about users. This understanding is predominantly derived from a blend of demographic and psychographic data. Harnessing these insights allows us to craft AI prompts that are not just informative but also resonate deeply with users, leading to interactions that are both engaging and meaningful. This approach ensures that AI systems are not just reactive but proactive in addressing the specific needs and preferences of individuals.

Demographic data encompasses basic characteristics such as age, gender, occupation, and geographic location. These factors offer a foundational understanding of the user, providing context that can shape how AI systems tailor their responses. For example, an AI interacting with a teenager might use a more casual tone and include references relevant to youth culture, whereas an interaction with a professional might be more formal and focus on industry-specific terminology. By integrating demographic data, AI systems can adjust their language, examples, and overall approach to better align with the user's background, thereby increasing the relevance of the interaction.

Psychographic data, on the other hand, delves into the user's interests, values, attitudes, and lifestyle. This type of data provides a more nuanced view of the individual, revealing what drives their behaviors and preferences. For instance, if an AI knows that a user is passionate about environmental sustainability, it can tailor responses to emphasize eco-friendly practices or highlight green initiatives. Understanding a user's psychographic profile allows AI to engage on a more personal level, addressing their specific interests and concerns, which can significantly enhance the quality of the interaction.

Combining these two types of data creates a comprehensive picture of the user, enabling AI systems to craft prompts and responses that are both contextually and personally relevant. This personalization is crucial in fostering a deeper connection between the user and the AI. When users feel understood and valued, their satisfaction with the interaction increases, leading to more positive outcomes. For example, a personalized AI prompt that acknowledges a user's recent activities or preferences can make the interaction feel more natural and engaging, as opposed to a generic response that lacks relevance.

Furthermore, leveraging user insights can lead to more successful outcomes in various applications of AI. In customer service, for instance, a personalized approach can resolve issues more effectively by addressing the user's specific concerns and preferences. In educational technology, understanding a learner's background and interests can tailor the content to better suit their needs, thereby improving engagement and learning outcomes. In marketing and advertising, personalized AI prompts can lead to more effective campaigns by aligning with the target audience's values and interests.

In essence, the power of user understanding in AI interactions lies in the ability to transform data into meaningful, personalized experiences. By accurately interpreting both demographic and psychographic data, AI systems can craft prompts that are not only more relevant but also more engaging.

This tailored approach not only enhances user satisfaction but also drives better results across various applications. As AI continues to advance, prioritizing a deep understanding of users will be crucial in creating interactions that are both impactful and effective.

CHAPTER 5

REFINING PROMPTS FOR TARGETED OUTCOMES

Refining prompts is a critical component of optimizing interactions with AI systems, ensuring that they provide responses that are not only accurate but also relevant and actionable. The process of prompt refinement is both an art and a science, involving a strategic approach to crafting prompts that guide AI models toward delivering precise outcomes. This iterative process is fundamental for harnessing the full potential of AI in various applications, from customer service to creative writing and complex data analysis.

At its core, prompt refinement is about enhancing the clarity, specificity, and focus of the input given to an AI model. AI systems, particularly those based on advanced natural language processing, rely heavily on the quality of the input they receive to generate meaningful responses. The process begins with an understanding of how these models interpret and respond to language. AI models can process a wide range of inputs, but their outputs are highly sensitive to the nuances in wording, context, and structure of the prompts.

The need for prompt refinement arises from the inherent variability in AI language models. Even minor alterations in how a prompt is phrased or framed can lead to significantly different responses. For instance, a prompt that is too vague may produce generalized answers that lack the specificity needed for actionable insights, while a prompt that is overly detailed might constrain the AI's ability to provide creative or unexpected solutions. Therefore, refining prompts involves a delicate balance—fine-tuning them to be specific enough to guide the AI while leaving enough room for nuanced responses.

The refinement process is dynamic and iterative. It starts with an initial prompt, which is then tested and evaluated based on the AI's output. Feedback is crucial at this stage; users need to assess whether the responses align with their expectations and goals. If not, adjustments are made to the prompt, and the cycle continues until the desired outcome is achieved. This iterative process is not only about correcting errors but also about continuously improving the interaction to better meet the needs of the user.

Common techniques for prompt refinement include clarifying the language used, specifying the context or constraints, and breaking down complex queries into simpler components. For example, instead of asking a broad question like "Tell me about climate change," a more refined prompt would be "Explain the impact of climate change on coastal cities in the next 50 years." This refined prompt narrows the focus, providing the AI with a clearer direction and thus increasing the likelihood of receiving a relevant and detailed response.

Additionally, leveraging user feedback plays a significant role in prompt refinement. By systematically gathering and analyzing feedback on the effectiveness of different prompts, users can gain insights into how minor adjustments influence the AI's performance. This feedback loop allows for a more informed approach to prompt crafting and adjustment, leading to more effective and targeted outcomes.

Another important aspect of prompt refinement is incorporating contextual information. Providing context helps the AI model understand the specific situation or background related to the prompt, thereby enhancing the relevance of its responses. For instance, including information about the intended audience or the purpose of the query can help the AI tailor its answers more precisely.

In summary, refining prompts is an ongoing process of enhancement that requires a deep understanding of how AI models interpret language and an iterative approach to fine-tuning inputs. By focusing on clarity, specificity, and context, and by utilizing feedback effectively, users can significantly improve the quality and relevance of AI responses. This chapter explores these techniques in detail, offering practical insights into how prompt refinement can lead to more targeted and actionable outcomes in AI interactions.

ANALYZING USER FEEDBACK FOR PROMPT IMPROVEMENT

User feedback is an invaluable asset for refining AI prompts, enabling a more effective interaction between users and the AI. This feedback can be divided into two main types: implicit and explicit. Both types offer distinct insights into how well the prompts are performing and where improvements can be made.

Implicit and Explicit User Feedback

Implicit feedback refers to the indirect signals users give through their interactions with the AI. For example, if users frequently modify their questions or show patterns of disengagement after receiving responses, it indicates potential shortcomings in the prompts. Such behavior might suggest that the prompts are not eliciting the desired responses or that users are not finding the answers relevant or useful. By analyzing these patterns, developers can infer areas where the prompts may need to be adjusted.

On the other hand, explicit feedback is more direct and involves users actively providing their opinions about the AI's responses. This can include user ratings, comments, or structured surveys where users assess the quality and relevance of the answers they receive. Explicit feedback allows for a more straightforward assessment of prompt effectiveness, as users can directly communicate their satisfaction or dissatisfaction.

To effectively utilize user feedback for prompt improvement, it is crucial to analyze both types of feedback comprehensively. Identifying recurring issues or trends in implicit feedback and combining these with explicit feedback helps in understanding specific areas of user frustration or confusion. For instance, if users consistently rate a particular type of response poorly, it might indicate a need to refine the prompt to better capture the user's intent or provide more precise guidance.

Improving Prompts Based on Feedback

Once feedback is collected, the next step is to analyze it to identify patterns and areas for improvement. This process involves examining the feedback for common themes, such as frequently misunderstood queries or areas where responses are deemed unsatisfactory. Based on these insights, developers can refine prompts to make them clearer and more aligned with user needs. This might involve rephrasing prompts to eliminate ambiguity, adding context where needed, or breaking down complex queries into simpler components.

Additionally, feedback analysis can reveal gaps in the AI's knowledge or areas where its understanding of user intent may be lacking. By addressing these gaps, developers can enhance the AI's ability to generate relevant and accurate responses, thus improving overall user satisfaction.

IDENTIFYING AND CORRECTING COMMON PROMPTING MISTAKES

Effective prompt design is essential for generating accurate and useful AI responses. Common mistakes in prompt design can significantly impact the quality of the responses, making it crucial to identify and correct these issues.

Misalignment with User Needs

One of the most prevalent issues in prompt design is misalignment with user needs. This occurs when prompts are not well-aligned with what users are actually seeking. For instance, if a prompt is framed too generally or ambiguously, the AI might generate responses that do not meet the user's specific expectations or goals. Identifying misalignment involves closely analyzing user feedback and understanding the outcomes users are aiming for. This process helps in adjusting the prompts to better reflect the user's intent and provide more relevant answers.

Too Broad or Narrow Prompts

Another common issue is creating prompts that are either too broad or too narrow. Broad prompts can lead to overly general responses that lack the specificity users need, while narrow prompts might restrict the AI's ability to provide a comprehensive answer. Striking the right balance is essential. To address this, developers can refine prompts by adding necessary context, specifying key details, or breaking down broader queries into smaller, more targeted questions. This helps in generating responses that are both relevant and sufficiently detailed to meet user needs.

In conclusion, analyzing user feedback is crucial for refining AI prompts and enhancing the overall user experience. By understanding and correcting common prompting mistakes, developers can create more effective and user-centered AI interactions, leading to improved satisfaction and engagement.

The Role of Context in Prompting

Context is a fundamental element in the interaction between users and AI systems. The effectiveness of an AI's response is heavily reliant on the clarity and relevance of the context provided within a prompt. Context helps the AI understand not only the surface-level request but also the underlying nuances and intent behind it. This allows the AI to generate responses that are more accurate, relevant, and meaningful to the user.

BUILDING CONTEXT WITH FOLLOW-UP PROMPTS

Building context with follow-up prompts is a strategic approach to refining the AI's responses. Initially, a broad or general prompt may be used to gauge the AI's understanding of a topic. Once the AI provides an initial response, users can introduce follow-up prompts that add more specific details or clarify aspects of the topic. This iterative process allows users to narrow down the focus, gradually guiding the AI toward the desired depth and specificity.

For example, if a user is seeking advice on improving their public speaking skills, an initial prompt might ask, "What are some tips for public speaking?" The AI might provide general advice on posture, voice modulation, and engaging the audience. To refine the response, the user could follow up with more targeted prompts like, "What are effective techniques for dealing with stage fright?" or "Can you provide strategies for improving speech structure?" Each follow-up prompt helps to build on the previous response, making the overall interaction more tailored and valuable.

This iterative approach not only enhances the relevance of the AI's answers but also enables users to address complex or multi-faceted queries incrementally. It encourages a dialogue-like exchange, where each prompt contributes to a deeper understanding of the topic.

Avoiding Context Confusion

While building context through follow-up prompts is beneficial, users must also be cautious to avoid context confusion. Introducing excessive or unrelated information can lead to responses that are disjointed or less relevant. Maintaining coherence in the context is essential for ensuring that the AI remains focused on the primary topic of interest. For instance, if a user begins by asking about effective strategies for team management and then abruptly shifts to a question about dietary habits, the AI may struggle to connect these topics if not clearly framed. This could lead to disjointed or confused responses, detracting from the usefulness of the interaction.

To avoid such issues, users should ensure that each follow-up prompt logically builds on the preceding one. It's important to keep the conversation coherent by relating new information back to the original query or clearly indicating when a shift in topic is intentional. For example, if discussing team management and shifting to dietary habits, users should explicitly state the connection, such as exploring how dietary habits can impact team productivity.

Additionally, providing context when introducing new topics can help maintain clarity. Users might state, "I'd like to shift to a different topic now" or "Building on our discussion about team management, I want to explore how health affects work performance." This approach helps the AI transition smoothly and maintain relevance in its responses.

In a nutshell, context plays a pivotal role in how effectively an AI can respond to prompts. By strategically building context with follow-up prompts, users can guide the AI toward more precise and relevant answers. However, it is equally important to avoid introducing unrelated or excessive context, which can lead to confusion and reduce the quality of the responses. Effective use of context involves a balance— ensuring clarity and relevance throughout the interaction to achieve the most useful outcomes.

LAYERING INFORMATION: CRAFTING MULTI-STEP PROMPTS

In the realm of interacting with AI, especially when tackling intricate or multifaceted inquiries, layering information through multi-step prompts is a strategic approach that can significantly enhance the quality and relevance of responses. By decomposing a query into smaller, logically sequenced components, users can guide the AI through a structured thought process, ensuring that each aspect of the query is addressed comprehensively before synthesizing a final response. This method not only improves clarity but also helps in managing complex information more effectively.

Step-by-Step Instructions

When faced with complex tasks, breaking them down into step-by-step instructions allows the AI to handle each element methodically. This approach is particularly valuable when a response requires multi-stage reasoning or a series of sequential actions. For instance, if a user needs help developing a business plan, instead of asking the AI to generate the entire plan in one go, they could first ask for a market analysis, then request a financial forecast, followed by an outline of the marketing strategy. By focusing on each stage separately, the AI can provide detailed and accurate information tailored to each component.

Step-by-step instructions are beneficial in several ways:

Clarity and Precision: By isolating each task, users ensure that the AI's focus remains on one aspect at a time, reducing the likelihood of overlooking important details.

Manageability: Complex queries become more manageable when divided into smaller parts, making it easier to track progress and adjust the approach if necessary.

Enhanced Understanding: This method allows the AI to build on previous responses, creating a coherent and well-structured final output that integrates insights from each step.

For example, if a user is looking for guidance on writing a research paper, a multi-step prompt might start with asking for advice on formulating a research question, followed by a discussion on gathering sources, then drafting an outline, and finally tips on revising and editing. This structured approach ensures that each stage of the writing process is addressed comprehensively.

Conditional Prompting

Conditional prompting introduces a layer of sophistication by creating scenarios where the AI must respond based on predefined conditions. This technique allows users to tailor responses more precisely by specifying different pathways the AI should follow depending on whether certain criteria are met. For instance, a user might instruct the AI to provide one type of answer if a user's input is a question about a product's features and another type if it's a question about product pricing.

Conditional prompting offers several advantages.

Nuanced Responses: By setting conditions, users enable the AI to produce responses that are contextually appropriate, enhancing the relevance and specificity of the output.

Dynamic Interaction: This method allows for more dynamic and flexible interactions, as the AI can adapt its responses based on real-time inputs and changing scenarios.

Improved User Experience: Tailoring responses based on conditions ensures that users receive the most pertinent information, improving overall satisfaction and effectiveness.

For example, in a customer support setting, a conditional prompt might direct the AI to offer troubleshooting steps if a user describes a technical problem or escalate the issue to a human agent if the problem is complex or unresolved by standard procedures. This ensures that users receive the appropriate level of assistance based on their specific needs.

In a nutshell, layering information through step-by-step instructions and conditional prompting allows users to navigate complex queries more effectively. By breaking down tasks into manageable components and tailoring responses based on conditions, users can enhance the accuracy, relevance, and utility of AI-generated outputs. This approach not only improves the AI's ability to handle intricate tasks but also provides users with a more organized and insightful interaction.

USING CONSTRAINTS TO GUIDE AI RESPONSES

Constraints are powerful tools for refining the output of AI systems. They function as a guiding framework, ensuring that the AI's responses are relevant, precise, and aligned with user expectations. By setting clear boundaries, constraints help in honing the focus of the AI, thereby preventing it from delivering information that is either too broad or irrelevant. Constraints can come in various forms, including limitations on tone, time, or length, each serving a unique purpose in shaping the AI's responses.

Setting Boundaries in Prompts

One of the primary ways to implement constraints is through the strategic design of prompts. Setting boundaries in prompts involves defining the scope and content of the AI's response to ensure it remains pertinent and on-topic. For example, a prompt that specifies "Explain the causes of climate change without discussing solutions" directs the AI to focus solely on the causes, thereby avoiding tangential discussions about potential remedies. This kind of precise direction helps the AI concentrate on delivering targeted information that aligns with the user's needs.

Explicit boundaries can also help in filtering out irrelevant information. When a prompt includes constraints such as "Provide a summary of the latest research on renewable energy, excluding historical data," it prevents the AI from providing outdated or irrelevant background information. By clearly defining what should or shouldn't be included, users can achieve more accurate and useful responses. This approach is particularly beneficial in academic, technical, or professional contexts where specificity and relevance are crucial.

Using Time, Tone, and Length Constraints

Constraints on time, tone, and length are instrumental in fine-tuning AI responses to match specific contexts and desired outcomes. These constraints ensure that the responses are not only relevant but also appropriately tailored to the user's requirements.

Time Constraints: Time constraints are used to manage the duration or speed of the response. For example, a prompt might request, "Summarize this document in under two minutes." This constraint ensures that the AI delivers a concise summary that captures the essence of the document without going into excessive detail. Time constraints are particularly useful in scenarios where quick decision-making is necessary, such as in business meetings or emergency situations.

Tone Constraints: The tone of the response is another crucial aspect influenced by constraints. A prompt like "Respond in a formal tone" directs the AI to use professional language and avoid casual expressions. Conversely, a prompt asking for a "friendly and conversational tone" encourages a more relaxed and approachable style. Adjusting the tone helps in aligning the AI's output with the context of the communication, whether it's a business report, a customer service interaction, or a casual blog post.

Length Constraints: Length constraints dictate the amount of detail provided in the response. For instance, "Limit your response to 200 words" ensures that the AI does not produce overly verbose or meandering answers. Length constraints are particularly useful when brevity is important, such as in executive summaries, briefings, or social media content. They help in maintaining clarity and focus, allowing users to digest information quickly without being overwhelmed.

In a nutshell, constraints are essential tools for guiding AI responses, helping to maintain focus, relevance, and appropriateness. By setting clear boundaries in prompts and using time, tone, and length constraints, users can significantly enhance the quality and utility of the AI's output. These strategies not only ensure that the information provided meets specific needs but also facilitate efficient communication and decision-making in various contexts.

TESTING AND ITERATING ON PROMPTS

Prompt refinement is an ongoing process that is crucial for optimizing the performance and relevance of AI systems. Unlike a static, one-time setup, effective prompt engineering involves continuous testing and iteration to ensure that prompts are adaptable and produce accurate, relevant, and efficient responses across various contexts.

1. The Necessity of Continuous Testing

Testing prompts with diverse user types and scenarios is essential for creating a robust AI interaction model. Users come with different expectations, backgrounds, and needs, which means that a single prompt may not work universally. For instance, a prompt designed for a technical support chatbot may need to be adjusted when addressing general customer service inquiries. By systematically testing prompts in varied situations, developers can identify and address potential issues, ensuring that the AI performs well in a wide array of contexts.

2. Methods of Prompt Testing

One effective method for testing prompts is A/B testing, which involves comparing two or more versions of a prompt to determine which one yields better results. This approach allows for a controlled comparison of prompt effectiveness by measuring performance metrics such as user satisfaction, accuracy of responses, or engagement levels. For instance, if a prompt is designed to elicit detailed information from users, A/B testing can reveal which version of the prompt results in more comprehensive and relevant responses.

Another valuable method is user feedback, which provides insights directly from the end-users interacting with the AI system. Feedback loops enable developers to gather qualitative data on how prompts are perceived and how well they meet user needs. This can include direct feedback from users or indirect metrics such as response times and the frequency of follow-up queries. Integrating user feedback into the prompt refinement process helps ensure that prompts are not only effective but also aligned with user expectations and preferences.

3. Iterative Refinement

Prompt refinement is an iterative process, meaning that adjustments and improvements are made based on the outcomes of testing and feedback. This iterative approach allows for incremental enhancements rather than large-scale overhauls, which can be more manageable and less disruptive. For instance, if a prompt is found to be causing confusion among users, developers might adjust the wording slightly or provide additional context rather than completely redesigning the prompt.

4. Evaluating Prompt Effectiveness

To ensure that prompts are continuously improved, it is important to evaluate their effectiveness through various metrics. Accuracy measures how well the AI's responses align with the intended outcomes of the prompt. Relevance assesses whether the responses are pertinent to the user's query or situation. Efficiency looks at how quickly and seamlessly the prompt generates appropriate responses. By regularly assessing these factors, developers can make data-driven decisions to refine prompts and enhance the overall user experience.

5. Addressing Diverse Use Cases

Prompts need to be versatile to accommodate diverse use cases. For example, a prompt intended for a healthcare chatbot might require different phrasing and sensitivity compared to a prompt for a travel booking assistant. Testing prompts across these varied scenarios helps ensure that the AI can handle a wide range of interactions effectively. This might involve creating specialized prompts for different contexts or adjusting general prompts to better suit specific situations.

6. The Role of Automated Tools

In addition to manual testing and feedback, automated tools can play a significant role in prompt refinement. These tools can simulate user interactions, analyze response patterns, and identify areas for improvement more efficiently than manual methods alone. By leveraging these tools, developers can expedite the testing process and gather comprehensive data on prompt performance.

So, prompt refinement is a dynamic and ongoing process that requires regular testing and iteration. By employing methods such as A/B testing, user feedback, and automated tools, developers can continuously improve prompts to ensure they are effective, relevant, and adaptable to a variety of use cases. This iterative approach not only enhances the quality of AI interactions but also contributes to a more satisfying user experience.

EXAMPLES: OPTIMIZING PROMPTS FOR VARIED SCENARIOS

This section explores how different strategies for refining prompts can enhance the performance of AI systems across various contexts. By delving into case studies that contrast simple versus complex queries and examining user-specific prompting techniques, we can better understand how tailored prompts improve AI responsiveness and accuracy.

Simple Queries vs. Complex Queries

Simple Queries:

Simple queries are straightforward requests that typically involve single-step tasks, such as asking for a definition or a fact. For example, asking "What is the capital of France?" is a simple query. These types of queries often require minimal refinement because the response is clear-cut and does not depend on multiple variables or layers of information. The AI system can provide a direct answer without needing to interpret complex context or handle extensive details.

However, even with simple queries, there is room for optimization. Ensuring that the prompt is as specific as possible can help avoid ambiguity. For instance, instead of asking, "Tell me about Python," specifying "Tell me about the programming language Python" directs the AI to focus on the intended topic rather than potential other meanings of the term "Python," such as the reptile.

Complex Queries:

In contrast, complex queries involve multiple variables or steps and thus require more sophisticated prompting strategies. For instance, asking, "Can you help me plan a vacation?" involves several layers, including destination preferences, budget constraints, and travel dates. To manage this complexity, breaking the prompt into smaller, sequential questions can be more effective. For example:

1. "What are some popular vacation destinations in Europe?"
2. "Can you suggest activities for a family with young children?"
3. "What is a reasonable budget for a 7-day trip to one of these destinations?"

By decomposing the query, the AI can address each component individually, leading to more precise and useful responses. This method also allows users to refine their requests based on initial answers, ensuring that the final output aligns more closely with their needs.

Layered Prompts:

Another approach for complex queries is to use layered prompts that build on previous responses. For example, if a user asks for help with "finding the best marketing strategy for a new product," the AI might first inquire about the product's target audience and industry specifics. Once these details are provided, the AI can then offer tailored marketing strategies, making the advice more relevant and actionable.

User-Specific Prompting Examples: Technical Experts vs. Beginners:

User-specific prompting involves tailoring the complexity and detail of the prompt based on the user's background and expertise. For instance, a technical expert seeking advice on a coding problem might appreciate a prompt that includes specific technical jargon and in-depth analysis. An example prompt might be: "Can you explain the differences between deep learning architectures like CNNs and RNNs for time series prediction?"

In contrast, a beginner might need a more fundamental explanation. The same topic could be approached with a prompt like: "Can you describe what a convolutional neural network is and how it helps with analyzing images?"

By adjusting the prompt to match the user's level of expertise, the AI can provide responses that are neither too simplistic nor too complex, making the information more useful and accessible.

Contextual and Purpose-Driven Prompts

The context and purpose of the query also play a crucial role in prompt optimization. For example, a user asking for travel advice might need different levels of detail based on whether they are planning a luxury vacation or a budget trip. A prompt for a luxury vacation could be: "Can you recommend high-end accommodations and exclusive experiences in Tokyo?" Meanwhile, a budget-conscious traveler might ask: "What are some affordable yet enjoyable things to do in Tokyo?"

Refining prompts based on the intended use helps ensure that the AI's responses are tailored to meet specific needs and preferences, enhancing overall satisfaction and effectiveness.

Optimizing prompts for varied scenarios involves understanding the complexity of the query and the specific needs of the user. By distinguishing between simple and complex queries and adapting prompts based on user expertise, one can significantly improve the relevance and quality of AI-generated responses.

SUMMARY: MASTERING THE ART OF PROMPT REFINEMENT

Mastering the art of prompt refinement is a dynamic and ongoing process, crucial for achieving optimal interactions with AI systems. It is a sophisticated skill that encompasses understanding and applying principles of clarity, context, and iteration to craft prompts that elicit accurate and useful responses from artificial intelligence.

1. Clarity in Prompt Design

The foundation of effective prompt refinement lies in clarity. Clear prompts eliminate ambiguity and guide the AI toward producing precise and relevant responses. To achieve clarity, users must be specific about what they want the AI to address. This involves avoiding vague language and providing detailed instructions that leave little room for misinterpretation. For instance, instead of asking "Tell me about climate change," a more refined prompt would be,

"Explain the impact of climate change on polar ice caps and sea levels over the past decade." Such specificity helps the AI to focus on relevant information, thereby enhancing the quality of the response.

2. Contextual Awareness

Context is another critical component in prompt refinement. Providing context helps the AI understand the background and nuances of the query, leading to more accurate and contextually appropriate responses. Contextual prompts might include relevant background information, the intended audience, or the purpose of the query. For example, if a user needs information for a scientific paper, the prompt might include details about the paper's topic, target audience, and the level of technical detail required. Contextual prompts ensure that the AI's output aligns with the user's expectations and needs.

3. Iterative Refinement

The process of prompt refinement is inherently iterative. Initial prompts often require adjustments based on the AI's responses. This iterative process involves reviewing the output, identifying areas for improvement, and modifying the prompt accordingly. For instance, if an AI's response is too broad or misses key details, the prompt can be revised to include more specific instructions or questions. This continuous cycle of refinement allows users to hone their prompts until they achieve the desired level of precision and relevance.

4. Leveraging User Feedback

User feedback is invaluable in refining prompts. Collecting and analyzing feedback from interactions with the AI provides insights into how well the prompts are functioning and where adjustments are needed. Feedback might reveal common issues, such as misunderstood queries or recurring errors, which can then be addressed in subsequent prompt refinements. Engaging with users to gather their experiences and suggestions helps in crafting prompts that are more effective and aligned with their expectations.

5. Avoiding Common Mistakes

Awareness of common mistakes in prompt design can also enhance the refinement process. Common errors include overly complex language, lack of specificity, and failure to account for the AI's limitations. Simplifying language, clearly defining objectives, and recognizing the boundaries of the AI's capabilities are essential steps in avoiding these pitfalls. For example, prompts that are too complex or layered may confuse the AI, leading to less coherent responses. By addressing these mistakes, users can create more effective and targeted prompts.

6. Employing Multi-Step and Constrained Prompts

Multi-step prompts, which break down complex queries into smaller, manageable parts, can improve the AI's ability to provide detailed and accurate responses. Constrained prompts, which limit the scope of the response, can help in focusing the AI's output on specific aspects of the query. Both approaches contribute to more effective prompt refinement by guiding the AI's focus and reducing the likelihood of irrelevant or excessive information.

In a nutshell, mastering the art of prompt refinement is an ongoing journey of learning and adaptation. By emphasizing clarity, context, and iterative improvement, and by leveraging user feedback and avoiding common mistakes, users can significantly enhance AI performance. The key takeaway is that prompt refinement is a dynamic process that requires continuous adjustments and improvements to meet evolving user needs and harness the full potential of AI capabilities.

CHAPTER 6

SAMPLES PROMPTS FOR TARGETED OUTCOMES

CV Prompt

"I want you to produce a comprehensive CV for me using these information, Name: [Your Full Name]
Contact Information: [Phone Number, Email Address]
Professional Summary: [Brief overview of your career goals and key qualifications]
Experience:
1. Job Title: [Your Job Title]
   Company: [Company Name]
   Dates: [Start Date – End Date]
   Responsibilities in 50 words: [Key Responsibilities and Achievements]
2. Job Title: [Your Job Title]
   Company: [Company Name]
   Dates: [Start Date – End Date]
   Responsibilities: [Key Responsibilities and Achievements]

Education:
Degree: [Your Degree]
Institution: [Institution Name]
Year of Graduation: [Year]
Skills: [Relevant Skills and Certifications]
References: [Available upon request]"

You can adjust sections based on your experience and career stage.

Cover Letter Prompt

"Create a CV cover letter for a [Job Title] position at [Company Name]. Highlight my relevant experience, including [Specific Experience or Skill]. Address the letter to [Hiring Manager's Name], emphasizing why my background in [Relevant Field/Industry] aligns with the job requirements listed in the description [Paste Job Requirement]. Include a summary of my accomplishments in [Relevant Skills or Achievements]."

Personal Statement Prompt

"Craft a personal statement for a [Job Title] position at [Company Name]. Highlight my experience in [Relevant Experience], emphasizing skills such as [Key Skills]. Relate my background to the roles and responsibilities outlined in the job description [Input Job description/Requirement], specifically focusing on how my expertise aligns with the company's needs and goals."

Here are 200 prompt samples to help content creators maximize their use of ChatGPT

Content Ideation & Strategy

1. "Generate 10 blog post ideas on [topic]."
2. "What are some content ideas for promoting a [type of product]?"
3. "Give me a list of social media post ideas for [industry]."
4. "What are some trending topics in [industry] right now?"
5. "Suggest a content calendar for the next month on [topic]."
6. "How can I repurpose my blog post on [topic] for social media?"
7. "What content types resonate most with [audience demographic]?"
8. "What are some unique angles for writing about [topic]?"
9. "Give me ideas for an Instagram reel related to [subject]."
10. "Generate 5 potential podcast episode titles about [topic]."
11. "What are some evergreen content topics in [industry]?"
12. "Suggest some YouTube video ideas to target [audience]."
13. "Provide ideas for a series of LinkedIn posts about [industry trend]."
14. "What type of visual content performs well in the [industry] space?"
15. "Create a list of lead magnets for my [type of business]."
16. "What are the best content pillars for a [type of brand]?"
17. "Generate ideas for case study topics related to [product/service]."
18. "Provide 5 ideas for interactive social media content on [platform]."
19. "How can I use humor in my content around [topic]?"
20. "Suggest a content theme for each quarter of the year focused on [topic]."

Content Writing & Copywriting

21. "Write an engaging blog post introduction about [topic]."
22. "How can I write a compelling call to action for [specific product]?"
23. "Write a persuasive product description for [product name]."
24. "Create a catchy headline for a blog post about [topic]."
25. "Write a closing paragraph for an article on [subject]."
26. "Generate 10 attention-grabbing blog post titles about [subject]."
27. "How can I make my writing more relatable to [audience]?"
28. "Rewrite this sentence to sound more engaging: '[sentence]'."
29. "Create a short bio for an author writing about [subject]."
30. "Help me write a value proposition for my [product/ service]."
31. "Draft a thank-you email to customers after purchasing [product]."
32. "Write a concise product tagline for [business name]."
33. "How can I simplify complex technical language in my writing?"
34. "Create a comparison chart between [product A] and [product B]."
35. "Give me an example of a lead paragraph for an article on [topic]."
36. "Write a Facebook ad promoting [product/service]."
37. "Draft a promotional email for my latest [product/offer]."
38. "Create a witty Twitter post about [industry trend]."
39. "How can I optimize my blog post for SEO on [keyword]?"
40. "Help me write a blog post conclusion on [topic]."

SEO & Optimization

41. "Give me a list of high-traffic keywords related to [topic]."
42. "What are long-tail keywords I can target for [subject]?"
43. "How can I optimize my website content for [specific SEO goal]?"
44. "Generate meta descriptions for a blog post on [topic]."
45. "What are the most important on-page SEO factors for [industry]?"
46. "How can I improve my click-through rate for articles on [topic]?"
47. "Provide me with a content structure optimized for [keyword]."
48. "What internal links should I add to this article on [topic]?"
49. "Give me ideas for optimizing image alt tags on my website."
50. "Suggest ways to optimize my blog post for voice search on [subject]."
51. "What SEO mistakes should I avoid in my content strategy?"
52. "Generate a list of backlinks opportunities in the [niche] industry."
53. "How can I improve my site's domain authority using content?"
54. "What are some effective content optimization tools for SEO?"
55. "What are some content distribution channels that can boost my SEO?"
56. "How can I write blog posts that rank on the first page for [keyword]?"
57. "Provide a sample blog outline optimized for [SEO keyword]."
58. "What LSI (Latent Semantic Indexing) keywords can I use for [topic]?"
59. "Write an SEO-friendly URL for a blog post on [subject]."
60. "How can I improve my content readability for SEO?"

Engagement & Audience Interaction

61. "What are effective ways to engage my [target audience] on [platform]?"
62. "Create a poll question I can ask on Instagram Stories related to [topic]."
63. "Suggest interactive content ideas for boosting engagement with [audience]."
64. "What are some effective ways to respond to comments on my blog?"
65. "Give me ideas for a user-generated content campaign for [brand]."
66. "How can I encourage more social shares for my content on [platform]?"
67. "Write a personalized reply to a customer asking about [product]."
68. "What are the best ways to spark a conversation around [topic] on Twitter?"
69. "How can I increase engagement on my [platform] account?"
70. "Generate 5 questions I can ask my audience to prompt engagement on [topic]."
71. "Create an engaging CTA for my followers to comment on [type of post]."
72. "Suggest some fun Instagram Story ideas for [type of business]."
73. "How can I turn a negative comment on my post about [topic] into a positive?"
74. "Create an outline for a Q&A session around [topic]."
75. "What are some creative ways to ask for feedback from my audience?"
76. "How can I involve my community more in content creation?"
77. "Generate a list of hashtags I can use to reach a larger audience on [platform]."

78. "What are some ways to humanize my brand's social media presence?"
79. "Write a prompt for my audience to share their experiences with [product/service]."
80. "Suggest a series of challenge-based posts that would encourage user participation."

Creative Inspiration & Visual Content

81. "What visual elements can I add to my blog post about [topic]?"
82. "Suggest some aesthetic color palettes for a [type of brand]."
83. "Generate an infographic idea on [topic]."
84. "What are some creative visual content ideas for promoting [product]?"
85. "Create a storyboard for an explainer video about [subject]."
86. "What are some trending design styles for Instagram posts?"
87. "Suggest visuals that would complement an article on [subject]."
88. "Give me ideas for a branded Instagram carousel post on [topic]."
89. "Help me design an appealing email newsletter layout."
90. "What visual content works best for engaging [audience demographic]?"
91. "Create a wireframe for a landing page focused on [product]."
92. "What type of graphics can I use to boost engagement in [industry]?"
93. "How can I create a visually appealing content grid for Instagram?"
94. "Generate creative ideas for a [type of brand] video ad campaign."

95. "What are some best practices for designing clickable Pinterest pins?"
96. "How can I incorporate user-generated visuals into my content strategy?"
97. "Give me suggestions for creating an aesthetically pleasing YouTube thumbnail."
98. "What are some effective tips for combining visuals and copy in [content type]?"
99. "What photography styles work well for [type of brand] content?"
100. "How can I make my website visually engaging to retain visitors?"

Content Promotion & Distribution

101. "What are the best channels for promoting content in [industry]?"
102. "How can I promote my blog post on [topic] across different platforms?"
103. "What are some content syndication platforms for republishing articles?"
104. "Write a brief for a Facebook ad campaign promoting [content type]."
105. "How can I boost the organic reach of my content on [social platform]?"
106. "Suggest promotional strategies for my eBook about [topic]."
107. "Create a content distribution checklist for my [type of content]."
108. "How can I leverage influencer marketing to promote [content or product]?"
109. "Write a social media post that teases my upcoming blog on [subject]."
110. "What email marketing strategies can I use to promote my latest post?"

111. "Give me strategies for cross-promoting my YouTube videos on [other platform]."
112. "How can I build partnerships with other creators to promote [content]?"
113. "What are some creative ways to collaborate with influencers in [industry]?"
114. "Suggest a weekly content distribution plan for [content type]."
115. "How can I create an effective social media ad for promoting [content]?"
116. "What's the best way to use email newsletters to share my content?"
117. "What are some paid advertising platforms I can use to boost [content]?"
118. "Write an outreach email to promote my guest blog post on [topic]."
119. "What are the most effective ways to promote content through podcasts?"
120. "Suggest ways to use remarketing ads to promote my content."

Analysis & Improvement

121. "How can I measure the success of my content on [platform]?"
122. "What are the best metrics to track for content performance in [industry]?"
123. "Suggest ways to improve my content engagement on [platform]."
124. "What are some tools to analyze how well my content resonates with [audience]?"
125. "How can I use A/B testing to optimize my content strategy?"
126. "What are the common content creation mistakes to avoid in [industry]?"

127. "Analyze this social media post and suggest improvements: '[paste post].'"
128. "How can I use feedback to refine my content on [topic]?"
129. "What are the best ways to update outdated content on my website?"
130. "How can I track conversions from my blog posts?"
131. "What tools can I use to audit my content's SEO performance?"
132. "Suggest improvements to my content distribution strategy on [platform]."
133. "How can I test different content formats to see what works best for my audience?"
134. "Give me tips for improving the readability of my blog posts."
135. "What can I do to reduce bounce rates on my content?"
136. "Analyze the tone of my writing in this article and suggest tweaks."
137. "How can I increase the time visitors spend on my content?"
138. "Suggest methods to improve the visual hierarchy of my website content."
139. "What are the most common reasons for low engagement on content in [industry]?"
140. "Give me tips for making my content more shareable."

Content Monetization & Business Growth

141. "What are some ways to monetize my blog about [topic]?"
142. "How can I create a successful online course around [subject]?"
143. "Suggest ways to create paid membership content for [audience]."
144. "What are effective affiliate marketing strategies for content creators?"
145. "How can I use content marketing to boost sales for [product]?"

146. "Give me ideas for digital products I can create around [topic]."

147. "How can I monetize my YouTube channel focused on [subject]?"

148. "Suggest a content sales funnel for [type of product/ service]."

149. "What are some ways to create premium content for [target audience]?"

150. "How can I generate passive income from my [type of content]? "

151. "What are the best ways to sell online courses through content marketing?"

152. "Create a list of high-converting lead generation content ideas for [business]."

153. "How can I build a content strategy that drives more conversions?"

154. "What are some effective subscription models for monetizing content?"

155. "Write a product launch email to promote [new product]."

156. "How can I use sponsored content to grow my revenue in [niche]?"

157. "What types of exclusive content can I offer for paid subscribers?"

158. "Generate ideas for digital downloads to sell on my website about [topic]."

159. "How can I use a blog to support my e-commerce business?"

160. "What are some ways to offer tiered content for different subscription levels?"

Content Automation & Workflow Efficiency

161. "What are the best tools for automating my content posting on [platform]?"

162. "How can I create a streamlined content creation workflow for [type of business]?"

163. "Give me tips for batch-creating social media posts efficiently."
164. "How can I automate my email marketing campaigns for content distribution?"
165. "What tools can I use to manage multiple content creation projects?"
166. "Write a template for scheduling posts across different platforms."
167. "How can I use AI tools to assist with content research for [topic]?"
168. "What are some productivity hacks for content creators?"
169. "How can I outsource content creation while maintaining quality control?"
170. "Suggest a system for organizing my content ideas for future posts."
171. "How can I automate my content repurposing strategy?"
172. "Write a task list for launching a content campaign on [platform]."
173. "What content management systems are best for scaling my content business?"
174. "Suggest ways to improve collaboration with my content team."
175. "What are the best content curation tools for [industry]?"
176. "How can I automate tracking and reporting of my content performance?"
177. "Create a content calendar template for [type of business]."
178. "How can I integrate different content tools into one efficient workflow?"
179. "What tools help automate content idea generation for [topic]?"
180. "How can I streamline my content approval process with my team?"

Niche-Specific Content Creation

181. "What are some unique blog post ideas for a [type of business]?"
182. "Suggest engaging content for [specific holiday] for [industry]."
183. "How can I make [industry] content more exciting to my audience?"
184. "What are trending topics in [industry] that I can write about?"
185. "Give me a content marketing plan for a [type of business]."
186. "How can I position my content to stand out in the competitive [industry]?"
187. "What are some ideas for a YouTube channel focused on [niche]?"
188. "How can I make [industry] tutorials easy to follow for beginners?"
189. "Suggest fun ways to present [industry] statistics in content."
190. "Write a podcast script introduction for [industry topic]."
191. "How can I use storytelling to engage my audience in [industry]?"
192. "What are some popular content formats in the [industry] niche?"
193. "What are key trends in [industry] that I should focus my content on?"
194. "Create an outline for a webinar on [industry-related topic]."
195. "How can I use infographics to explain complex concepts in [industry]?"
196. "Suggest ideas for a case study on how [product] helps in [industry]."
197. "How can I educate my audience about [industry topic] using videos?"

198. "What are the most common challenges faced by content creators in [niche]?"
199. "What are creative ways to teach [industry topic] through content?"
200. "Suggest a content series for beginners entering [industry]."

Here are 50 detailed prompt samples that can help content creators maximize their use of ChatGPT. These prompts cover a wide range of tasks like brainstorming, content generation, editing, research, and more:

1. Content Idea Brainstorming
"Generate 10 unique blog post ideas for a travel blog targeting budget travelers. The posts should focus on tips, hidden gems, and underrated destinations. Include diverse regions such as Southeast Asia, South America, and Europe."

2. YouTube Script Outline
"Create a detailed outline for a 10-minute YouTube video on the topic of 'How to Stay Productive While Working from Home.' Break it into sections like introduction, key points, and conclusion, and suggest engaging visuals or examples to include."

3. Newsletter Ideas
"I need five engaging ideas for a weekly newsletter aimed at digital marketers. Topics should cover SEO strategies, social media trends, content marketing tips, and any upcoming events or tools worth highlighting."

4. Headline Variations

"Provide 10 attention-grabbing headline options for a blog post titled 'The Ultimate Guide to Vegan Nutrition.' Ensure that each headline is optimized for search engine clicks and appeals to a health-conscious audience."

5. Social Media Captions

"Generate 5 creative Instagram captions for a fashion brand promoting their new summer collection. Captions should be fun, trendy, and include a call to action for users to visit the online store."

6. Engagement-Boosting Questions

"Write 7 questions that I can ask my audience on Facebook to increase engagement and conversation. The questions should be related to self-improvement and productivity, appealing to an audience interested in personal growth."

7. SEO Keyword Ideas

"Suggest 15 long-tail keywords for a blog post on 'eco-friendly beauty products.' The keywords should have a balance of good search volume and low competition, and should include phrases relevant to sustainability and ethical sourcing."

8. Call-to-Action Examples

"Write 5 different versions of a call to action for a landing page offering a free downloadable e-book on 'Mastering Content Marketing.' The CTAs should encourage users to provide their email in exchange for the download."

9. Content Calendar Plan

"Create a content calendar for a month of blog posts for a tech blog. Include topics, brief descriptions of each post, and key dates that align with tech industry events or news. Posts should target both beginners and experts in technology."

10. Hashtag Suggestions
"Recommend 10 relevant hashtags for a Twitter campaign focused on spreading awareness about mental health. The hashtags should resonate with audiences interested in wellness, therapy, and breaking the stigma around mental health."

11. Podcast Episode Ideas
"Provide 7 creative episode ideas for a podcast about entrepreneurship. Each idea should focus on a specific aspect of business, such as marketing strategies, leadership, scaling a startup, or dealing with failure."

12. Email Subject Lines
"Write 10 catchy subject lines for a sales email promoting a summer sale on outdoor adventure gear. Ensure the subject lines are personalized, exciting, and include a sense of urgency to open."

13. Visual Content Ideas
"Suggest 5 ideas for visually engaging content that a lifestyle brand can share on Instagram Stories. Focus on ideas like user-generated content, behind-the-scenes footage, product demos, and interactive polls."

14. Content Repurposing
"How can I repurpose a 1,500-word blog post on 'The Benefits of Meditation' into different formats for social media, email newsletters, and a YouTube video? Provide specific ideas for repurposing across these platforms."

15. Tone of Voice Suggestions
"I need to adjust my blog's tone of voice to appeal more to millennials who are interested in sustainability. Suggest 5 ways to make my writing more relatable and approachable without losing its professional edge."

16. Explainer Video Script
"Write a script for a 2-minute explainer video introducing a new productivity app for freelancers. The script should focus on the app's key features, its ease of use, and how it helps streamline workflow."

17. Content Promotion Plan
"Create a step-by-step promotion plan for a blog post on 'How to Start a Successful Freelancing Career.' Include strategies for promoting on social media, through email marketing, and via collaboration with influencers or guest bloggers."

18. Audience Research
"Help me identify my target audience for an online course on 'Mastering Digital Marketing.' What demographic details should I focus on, and how can I find their pain points to tailor my course content to meet their needs?"

19. Blog Post Structure
"Outline a blog post structure for '5 Simple Ways to Reduce Your Carbon Footprint.' Include sections like introduction, key tips, statistics to support each point, and a conclusion with actionable steps."

20. Product Description Variations
"Write 3 different product descriptions for an eco-friendly water bottle. One should be concise for use on social media, one detailed for a product page, and one emotional, highlighting its impact on reducing plastic waste."

21. Case Study Outline
"Create a detailed outline for a case study on how a small business increased its online sales by 300% through content marketing. Include sections for the problem, the solution, strategies used, and measurable results."

22. Interview Questions
"Generate 10 thought-provoking interview questions for a guest on my podcast who specializes in personal finance for young adults. Focus on topics like budgeting, investing, and overcoming debt."

23. Personal Branding Advice
"Help me refine my personal brand as a motivational speaker. What key messages should I focus on, and how can I craft a narrative that resonates with an audience looking for guidance in achieving their life goals?"

24. Engaging Blog Introduction
"Write an engaging introduction for a blog post titled 'How to Overcome Imposter Syndrome as a New Entrepreneur.' Hook readers with a relatable scenario, and briefly introduce the steps they'll learn in the post."

25. Viral Content Ideas
"Suggest 5 ideas for creating viral content in the fitness niche. Ideas should be highly shareable and involve challenges, user-generated content, or trendy workout routines that can easily be adapted for TikTok."

26. Niche Research
"I want to start a blog about sustainable fashion. Provide a list of subtopics within this niche that are currently trending and can attract traffic, along with potential headlines or post ideas."

27. Audience Engagement Strategy
"What are 5 ways I can improve engagement with my audience on Instagram for my handmade jewelry business? Focus on community-building techniques like user-generated content, storytelling, and personalized interactions."

28. Editing and Refining Content
"Review the following paragraph of my blog post on healthy eating habits and provide suggestions to improve readability, flow, and engagement. Here's the paragraph: [insert paragraph]."

29. Customer Journey Map
"Create a customer journey map for an e-commerce website that sells eco-friendly home products. Include key stages like awareness, consideration, purchase, and retention, with examples of content that would be useful at each stage."

30. Problem-Solution Framework
"Help me craft a problem-solution framework for a blog post on 'Why Businesses Should Invest in Employee Wellness Programs.' Start with the problem and explain why it matters, followed by a detailed solution and examples."

31. Content Pillar Strategy
"I want to develop a content pillar strategy for my personal finance blog. Can you suggest 3 to 4 core topics that I should focus on, and how can I branch out from these topics to create smaller, related pieces of content?"

32. Brand Storytelling
"Write a compelling brand story for a small family-owned coffee shop that emphasizes its commitment to sustainability and fair trade practices. The story should evoke emotion and connect with customers who care about ethical consumption."

33. Community-Building Content
"Suggest 5 content ideas for building a strong community around a vegan lifestyle blog. Ideas should include ways to engage readers, promote discussions, and encourage sharing personal experiences or tips."

34. Content Collaboration Ideas
"I want to collaborate with influencers to promote my skincare brand. What are 5 creative ways I can partner with influencers for content creation, while making sure the content aligns with my brand values?"

35. Course Outline
"Help me create a course outline for 'Mastering Social Media Marketing.' The course should be broken into 8 modules, each covering a specific platform or strategy, and should include exercises or tasks for students to apply their learning."

36. Content Optimization for SEO
"Review the following blog post and suggest 5 ways to optimize it for SEO. Focus on improving keyword placement, meta descriptions, alt text for images, and any other factors that can enhance search engine ranking. [Insert blog post]."

37. Content Upgrade Ideas
"Suggest 3 content upgrade ideas for a blog post on '10 Tips for a Minimalist Lifestyle.' The upgrades should be valuable resources that encourage readers to subscribe, such as checklists, e-books, or printable guides."

38. Engaging Twitter Threads
"Create an engaging Twitter thread on '5 Mistakes to Avoid When Starting a New Business.' Each tweet in the thread should offer value, use a conversational tone, and encourage followers to reply or retweet."

39. Content Diversification
"How can I diversify my content as a personal development coach? I currently have a blog and a podcast. Suggest additional content formats or platforms I should explore to reach a wider audience, such as video or online courses."

40. Content Ideation for Blog Posts
"I'm creating a blog post for an audience of [audience type], aged [age], located in [location], who are interested in [psychographic data]. Can you provide me with 5 unique and engaging blog post ideas that align with their interests and help address their specific challenges or desires?"

41. Social Media Campaign Strategy
"I want to develop a social media campaign targeted at [audience type] in [location] who are primarily aged [age] and are motivated by [psychographic data]. What would be an effective content plan, including messaging ideas, post types, and engagement strategies, to attract and convert this audience?"

42. Video Script Outline
"I need an outline for a [length] video script designed for [audience type], aged [age], in [location], who resonate with [psychographic data]. The video should be informative, entertaining, and encourage viewers to [desired action]. Can you break it down into sections, with key talking points?"

43. Email Newsletter Ideas
"I'm working on a monthly email newsletter for [audience type] in [location], aged [age], with a focus on [psychographic data]. What are some unique content ideas, including article topics, tips, and calls-to-action, that would provide value and encourage engagement from this audience?"

44. Product Launch Announcement Copy

"Help me create a compelling product launch announcement for [audience type], aged [age], in [location], who care about [psychographic data]. The announcement should highlight the product's key features, its benefits to this audience, and include a clear call to action for [desired outcome]."

45. Podcast Episode Brainstorm

"I'm planning a podcast episode for [audience type], aged [age], located in [location], who are interested in [psychographic data]. Can you suggest episode themes, guest speaker ideas, and discussion points that will resonate with this audience and provide them with actionable takeaways?"

46. Website Copy Optimization

"Can you help me optimize the copy for a website aimed at [audience type], aged [age], in [location], with interests in [psychographic data]? The goal is to increase user engagement and conversions. Provide suggestions for improving headlines, calls-to-action, and any other areas that could better speak to this audience."

47. Webinar Title and Description

"I'm hosting a webinar for [audience type], aged [age], in [location], focused on [psychographic data]. Can you come up with a catchy title and a compelling description that will attract registrations and clearly communicate the value of attending the webinar?"

48. Content Calendar Planning
"I need help developing a content calendar for the next month, aimed at [audience type], aged [age], located in [location], who are interested in [psychographic data]. The calendar should include blog post ideas, social media content, and email topics, aligned with seasonal trends and this audience's preferences."

49. Landing Page Headline Testing
"I'm creating a landing page for [audience type], aged [age], in [location], whose motivations include [psychographic data]. Can you generate 5 alternative headlines that could increase conversions, each catering to a different aspect of what this audience finds important?"

50. Brand Voice Development
"I'm trying to develop a unique brand voice for a company that targets [audience type], aged [age], in [location], who are motivated by [psychographic data]. Could you provide some examples of how the brand voice should sound in blog posts, social media captions, and promotional emails to effectively connect with this audience?"

51. Affiliate Marketing Strategies
"Provide a detailed strategy for promoting affiliate products on a lifestyle blog. Include methods for integrating affiliate links naturally into content, tracking performance, and optimizing affiliate revenue."

52. Content Series Planning
"Help me plan a content series for a blog focused on personal finance for millennials. Outline the main theme of the series, and suggest 8 related blog post topics with brief descriptions for each."

53. Brand Ambassador Program
"Outline a strategy for creating a brand ambassador program for a new fitness apparel line. Include criteria for selecting ambassadors, ways to engage them, and incentives to keep them motivated."

54. Content Personalization
"Suggest 5 methods for personalizing content on an e-commerce website that sells kitchen gadgets. The suggestions should include techniques for using customer data to tailor recommendations and improve user experience."

55. Crisis Communication Plan
"Develop a crisis communication plan for a company that has received negative press. Outline steps for responding to the situation, including key messages, channels for communication, and ways to manage public relations."

56. Interactive Quiz Creation
"Design an interactive quiz for a health and wellness website. The quiz should be engaging, provide personalized results based on user answers, and include a call-to-action that leads to a related product or service."

57. E-book Creation
"Outline the structure for an e-book titled 'The Complete Guide to Remote Work Success.' Include chapters or sections, key topics to cover, and suggested content for each section, such as tips, case studies, and actionable advice."

58. Engaging Webinar Topics
"Suggest 5 compelling topics for webinars aimed at small business owners. Topics should address common challenges, provide practical solutions, and include ideas for interactive elements to keep attendees engaged."

59. Visual Content Design Tips

"Provide 7 tips for designing eye-catching visuals for a blog about home organization. Tips should cover aspects like color schemes, layout, typography, and image selection to enhance visual appeal and readability."

60. Customer Feedback Integration

"How can I effectively integrate customer feedback into my content strategy for an online course platform? Include methods for collecting feedback, analyzing it, and making content adjustments based on insights."

61. Product Launch Plan

"Create a detailed product launch plan for a new mobile app designed for fitness enthusiasts. Include steps for pre-launch marketing, launch day activities, and post-launch follow-up, with specific tactics for each phase."

62. Online Course Marketing

"Suggest 5 strategies for marketing an online course on 'Advanced SEO Techniques.' Strategies should include leveraging social media, partnerships, content marketing, and any other relevant channels to attract potential students."

63. Influencer Collaboration Tips

"Provide 5 tips for successfully collaborating with influencers in the travel niche. Tips should cover initial outreach, collaboration terms, content creation, and measuring the success of the partnership."

64. Content Distribution Strategy

"Develop a content distribution strategy for a new podcast about startup success stories. Include channels for promotion, tactics for reaching a wider audience, and methods for engaging listeners."

65. Market Research Methods
"Outline 5 effective market research methods for understanding consumer preferences in the beauty industry. Include both quantitative and qualitative techniques, and explain how the results can inform content creation."

66. Brand Consistency Guidelines
"Help me establish brand consistency guidelines for a new online coaching service. The guidelines should cover elements such as tone of voice, visual style, and messaging to ensure a cohesive brand identity across all platforms."

67. Content for Lead Generation
"Generate 5 content ideas specifically designed to capture leads for a software-as-a-service (SaaS) company. Ideas should focus on offering value to potential customers and include calls-to-action to encourage sign-ups."

68. Social Media Engagement Tactics
"Suggest 7 tactics for increasing engagement on LinkedIn for a B2B marketing agency. Tactics should include content ideas, interaction strategies, and ways to build professional relationships with potential clients."

69. Sales Copywriting Tips
"Provide 5 tips for writing persuasive sales copy for a new online course about personal development. Tips should focus on creating compelling headlines, addressing pain points, and crafting a strong call to action."

70. Content Collaboration Platforms
"Recommend 5 platforms or tools that facilitate content collaboration for a team working on a multi-author blog. Include features that support communication, version control, and project management."

71. Seasonal Content Ideas
"Suggest 6 seasonal content ideas for a lifestyle blog, focusing on topics related to fall. Include blog post ideas, social media content, and any special promotions or events that could be tied to the season."

72. Content Monetization Strategies
"Outline 5 strategies for monetizing a popular blog on parenting. Strategies should include options like affiliate marketing, sponsored content, and creating premium content or products for readers."

73. Content Syndication Plan
"Develop a plan for syndicating content from a tech blog to reach a broader audience. Include methods for identifying relevant platforms, establishing partnerships, and measuring the success of the syndication efforts."

74. User-Generated Content Campaign
"Create a plan for running a user-generated content campaign for a fitness brand. Include strategies for encouraging participation, guidelines for content submissions, and methods for showcasing user-generated content."

75. Brand Awareness Strategies
"Suggest 5 strategies for increasing brand awareness for a new eco-friendly product line. Strategies should include both online and offline methods, such as partnerships, influencer collaborations, and community engagement."

76. Content Performance Metrics
"Identify 6 key performance metrics for evaluating the success of a content marketing campaign. Explain what each metric measures, why it's important, and how to use the data to make informed decisions."

77. Email Marketing Campaign Ideas
"Propose 5 creative email marketing campaign ideas for a subscription box service that delivers gourmet snacks. Ideas should include themes, types of content to include, and strategies for increasing open and click-through rates."

78. Interactive Website Features
"Suggest 5 interactive features to add to a website for a home renovation company. Features should engage visitors, provide value, and encourage them to explore services or request a consultation."

79. Content Audit Checklist
"Create a checklist for conducting a content audit on a fashion blog. Include steps for evaluating content quality, performance metrics, SEO optimization, and opportunities for updating or repurposing existing content."

80. Brand Loyalty Programs
"Outline a strategy for developing a brand loyalty program for a high-end beauty brand. Include ideas for rewards, tiers of membership, and ways to encourage repeat purchases and customer referrals."

81. Storytelling Techniques
"Suggest 5 storytelling techniques for creating engaging content for a nonprofit organization focused on animal rescue. Techniques should help convey emotional impact, build connections with the audience, and drive support."

82. Content Creation Workflow
"Develop a workflow for creating content for a corporate blog. Include steps for ideation, research, writing, editing, and publishing, as well as methods for streamlining the process and ensuring consistency."

83. Competitive Analysis
"Perform a competitive analysis for a new online course on digital marketing. Identify key competitors, analyze their content strategies, and suggest opportunities for differentiating your course and capturing market share."

84. Content Curation Tips
"Provide 5 tips for effectively curating content for a weekly newsletter on industry trends. Tips should include sourcing quality content, maintaining relevance, and balancing curated content with original insights."

85. Customer Journey Mapping
"Create a customer journey map for an e-learning platform. Include stages from initial awareness through to post-purchase engagement, and suggest content and touchpoints that can improve the customer experience at each stage."

86. Web Content Optimization
"Suggest 5 ways to optimize web content for better user engagement and SEO performance. Focus on elements such as readability, keyword integration, multimedia use, and internal linking strategies."

87. Content Repurposing Strategy
"Develop a strategy for repurposing a popular webinar into various content formats, including blog posts, social media snippets, and downloadable resources. Include steps for adapting the content and promoting it across channels."

88. Influencer Outreach Email
"Write an outreach email template for contacting potential influencers to collaborate on promoting a new health and wellness product. The email should be personalized, concise, and include a clear value proposition for the influencer."

89. Content for Different Stages
"Suggest content ideas for a customer journey in an online fitness coaching business. Provide ideas for content that addresses awareness, consideration, and decision stages, including blog posts, videos, and lead magnets."

90. Brand Identity Development
"Help me develop a brand identity for a new pet care startup. Include elements such as brand values, mission statement, target audience, and key messaging that will resonate with pet owners."

91. Video Content Planning
"Create a plan for producing a series of instructional videos on 'Healthy Meal Prep for Busy Professionals.' Include video topics, content outlines, and ideas for visual and interactive elements to keep viewers engaged."

92. Content Promotion Tactics
"Suggest 5 tactics for promoting a new blog post about travel hacks on a shoestring budget. Tactics should include strategies for leveraging social media, email marketing, and partnerships with travel influencers."

93. Brand Message Refinement
"Help me refine the brand message for a new tech startup specializing in smart home devices. Focus on creating a clear, compelling message that highlights the company's unique selling points and appeals to tech-savvy consumers."

94. Content Scheduling Tools
"Recommend 5 content scheduling tools for managing a social media strategy for a fashion brand. Include features to look for, such as automation, analytics, and collaboration capabilities."

95. Blog Post Call-to-Action
"Write 3 different calls to action for a blog post about 'The Best Home Workouts for Beginners.' Each CTA should encourage readers to take a specific action, such as subscribing to a newsletter, downloading a guide, or joining a fitness challenge."

96. Customer Persona Development
"Create detailed customer personas for a new online marketplace for handmade crafts. Include demographic information, interests, pain points, and buying behaviors to help tailor content and marketing strategies."

97. Content Engagement Analysis
"Identify 5 key metrics for analyzing content engagement on a lifestyle blog. Explain how each metric can provide insights into reader behavior and content effectiveness, and how to use the data to improve future content."

98. Brand Storytelling Framework
"Develop a framework for storytelling that a startup can use to create compelling brand narratives. Include elements such as key story components, techniques for emotional connection, and tips for consistency across platforms."

99. Email List Growth Strategies
"Suggest 5 strategies for growing an email list for a tech blog. Include methods for capturing leads, such as offering incentives, creating engaging opt-in forms, and leveraging social media and partnerships."

100. Social Media Content Plan
"Create a social media content plan for a new gourmet coffee brand. Include a monthly calendar with post ideas, themes, and types of content to share on platforms like Instagram, Facebook, and Twitter."

Here are 50 detailed prompt samples on "Customer Persona Development" to help content creators make the most out of ChatGPT. Each prompt is designed to be adaptable with specific information:

1. "Describe a customer persona for a [product/service] aimed at [age group] who are interested in [specific interest]. Include their primary goals, pain points, and preferred communication channels."

2. "Create a detailed customer persona for a [brand] targeting [demographic] who frequently shops online. Outline their buying behavior, lifestyle choices, and the types of content they engage with most."

3. "Develop a persona for a [fitness product] consumer who values [specific feature]. What are their daily routines, major challenges related to fitness, and how do they seek solutions for their health and wellness?"

4. "Imagine a customer persona for a [technology gadget] used by [profession]. Describe their daily workflow, the technological problems they face, and what motivates them to adopt new gadgets."

5. "Outline a customer persona for a [luxury service] aimed at [income bracket] individuals. What are their primary values, spending habits, and preferred methods of discovering high-end services?"

6. "Create a persona for a [home decor] product consumer who lives in [type of home]. What are their design preferences, pain points related to home styling, and how do they typically research home decor ideas?"

7. "Design a customer persona for a [financial service] aimed at [age group] who are looking to invest. Include their financial goals, concerns about investment, and preferred sources of financial advice."

8. "Develop a persona for a [children's educational toy] buyer. What are their educational priorities for their children, how do they choose toys, and what factors influence their purchasing decisions?"

9. "Outline a persona for a [travel service] user who frequently travels for [specific reason]. What are their travel preferences, pain points during trips, and how do they typically plan their travel?"

10. "Create a detailed persona for a [sustainable product] consumer interested in [specific environmental issue]. What are their core values, daily habits related to sustainability, and how do they engage with eco-friendly brands?"

11. "Imagine a customer persona for a [personal development course] targeting [profession]. Describe their career goals, skill gaps they want to address, and their preferred learning methods."

12. "Develop a persona for a [health and wellness app] user who follows a [specific diet]. What are their health goals, challenges related to their diet, and how do they use apps to support their wellness journey?"

13. "Design a customer persona for a [pet product] aimed at [type of pet owner]. What are their pet care priorities, shopping habits for pet supplies, and the main factors they consider when buying products for their pet?"

14. "Outline a persona for a [new software] user in [industry]. What are their primary tasks, pain points with current software solutions, and what features do they prioritize in new software?"

15. "Create a detailed persona for a [fashion brand] customer who is passionate about [specific fashion trend]. What are their shopping habits, style preferences, and how do they stay updated on fashion trends?"

16. "Develop a persona for a [culinary product] consumer who loves [specific cuisine]. Describe their cooking habits, challenges in the kitchen, and what motivates them to try new culinary products."

17. "Design a customer persona for a [home improvement service] used by [homeowner type]. What are their renovation goals, pain points in home improvement, and how do they typically find and evaluate service providers?"

18. "Imagine a customer persona for a [music streaming service] user who enjoys [specific genre]. What are their listening habits, favorite features of music services, and how do they discover new music?"

19. "Outline a persona for a [digital marketing tool] user in [business size]. What are their marketing challenges, goals for digital campaigns, and what features do they find most valuable in digital marketing tools?"

20. "Create a detailed persona for a [beauty product] consumer who follows [specific beauty trend]. What are their skincare or makeup routines, pain points in beauty care, and how do they choose beauty products?"

21. "Develop a persona for a [financial planning service] client who is [career stage]. What are their long-term financial goals, concerns about retirement, and how do they seek financial planning advice?"

22. "Design a customer persona for a [fitness class] participant who is interested in [specific type of workout]. What are their fitness goals, challenges in sticking to a routine, and how do they find fitness classes?"

23. "Imagine a customer persona for a [subscription box] service focused on [specific interest]. What are their hobbies, preferred subscription features, and how do they decide which subscription boxes to try?"

24. "Outline a persona for a [professional development conference] attendee from [industry]. What are their career aspirations, learning objectives for the conference, and how do they engage with conference content?"

25. "Create a detailed persona for a [green energy product] consumer interested in [specific environmental impact]. What are their motivations for choosing green energy, challenges with adoption, and preferred information sources?"

26. "Develop a persona for a [luxury car] buyer who values [specific feature]. What are their car ownership habits, primary factors in purchasing decisions, and how do they research luxury vehicles?"

27. "Design a customer persona for a [tech startup] user who is [specific user type]. What are their technology needs, pain points with existing solutions, and how do they prefer to interact with tech startups?"

28. "Imagine a customer persona for a [personalized gift] buyer who is celebrating [specific occasion]. What are their gift-giving habits, challenges in finding personalized items, and how do they select gifts for special events?"

29. "Outline a persona for a [digital product] user interested in [specific function]. What are their usage habits, pain points with current digital tools, and what features do they wish to see in new digital products?"

30. "Create a detailed persona for a [premium skincare brand] customer who follows [specific skincare regimen]. What are their skincare concerns, buying behavior, and preferred ways to learn about new skincare products?"

31. "Develop a persona for a [family vacation package] purchaser interested in [specific destination]. What are their family vacation priorities, challenges in planning trips, and how do they choose vacation packages?"

32. "Design a customer persona for a [mobile app] user who enjoys [specific app function]. What are their daily app usage habits, issues with current apps, and what improvements would they like to see?"

33. "Imagine a customer persona for a [healthy snack] consumer who is [specific lifestyle]. What are their snacking habits, health goals, and how do they discover and select healthy snack options?"

34. "Outline a persona for a [home security system] user who is concerned about [specific security issue]. What are their security priorities, challenges with current solutions, and how do they evaluate home security systems?"

35. "Create a detailed persona for a [crafting product] enthusiast who loves [specific craft]. What are their crafting habits, challenges with materials, and how do they find inspiration and supplies for their projects?"

36. "Develop a persona for a [digital entertainment platform] user who is interested in [specific content type]. What are their content consumption habits, preferred features of digital platforms, and how do they discover new content?"

37. "Design a customer persona for a [budget travel service] user who travels to [specific destinations]. What are their travel budgeting strategies, pain points in finding affordable travel options, and how do they plan their trips?"

38. "Imagine a customer persona for a [personal fitness trainer] client who is focused on [specific fitness goal]. What are their workout preferences, challenges in achieving their goals, and how do they choose personal trainers?"

39. "Outline a persona for a [high-end gadget] enthusiast who is interested in [specific technology]. What are their tech interests, buying behavior, and how do they stay informed about the latest gadgets?"

40. "Create a detailed persona for a [wellness retreat] attendee interested in [specific wellness practice]. What are their wellness goals, challenges in maintaining wellness, and how do they choose retreat experiences?"

41. "Develop a persona for a [DIY home project] enthusiast who enjoys [specific type of project]. What are their project goals, challenges with DIY tasks, and how do they source materials and instructions?"

42. "Design a customer persona for a [subscription-based learning platform] user who is interested in [specific subject]. What are their learning goals, challenges in continuing education, and how do they select learning platforms?"

43. "Imagine a customer persona for a [luxury fashion item] buyer who values [specific feature]. What are their fashion priorities, shopping behavior, and how do they stay updated on luxury fashion trends?"

44. "Outline a persona for a [healthcare service] user who is focused on [specific health issue]. What are their healthcare needs, challenges in managing their health, and how do they choose healthcare services?"

45. "Create a detailed persona for a [tech accessory] buyer who uses [specific tech device]. What are their accessory needs, pain points with current accessories, and how do they select tech accessories?"

46. "Develop a persona for a [luxury travel experience] customer who is interested in [specific type of luxury

 travel]. What are their travel preferences, luxury criteria, and how do they plan and book luxury trips?"

47. "Design a customer persona for a [personal finance app] user interested in [specific financial goal]. What are their financial management habits, challenges with budgeting, and what features do they seek in finance apps?"

48. "Imagine a customer persona for a [premium subscription service] who is interested in [specific content or feature]. What are their subscription habits, content preferences, and how do they evaluate premium services?"

49. "Outline a persona for a [fitness equipment] buyer who is focused on [specific workout type]. What are their fitness goals, equipment needs, and how do they research and choose fitness equipment?"

50. "Create a detailed persona for a [high-tech kitchen appliance] user who enjoys [specific cooking style]. What are their cooking habits, challenges with current appliances, and what features do they prioritize in new kitchen technology?"

Feel free to modify the placeholders to fit your specific needs and objectives!

Certainly! Here are 20 detailed prompt samples for creating a company of one, where ChatGPT takes on specific job roles:

1. Marketing Specialist: "Imagine you are starting a solo business offering [specific product/service]. As the Marketing Specialist, create a detailed plan for launching your brand, including target audience analysis, social media strategy, and content calendar. How would you use [specific platform] to reach potential customers?"

2. Financial Planner: "You are running a one-person company focusing on [specific industry]. As the Financial Planner, outline your budget for the first year. Include projected income, expenses, and savings goals. How would you manage cash flow and handle unexpected costs?"

3. Customer Service Representative: "Your new business in [specific niche] requires exceptional customer service. As the Customer Service Representative, draft responses to three common customer inquiries or complaints. How would you ensure customer satisfaction and build a loyal client base?"

4. Content Creator: "Starting a one-person business in [specific field], you need to create engaging content. As the Content Creator, develop a content strategy for your blog, social media, and email marketing. What types of content will you produce, and how will you maintain consistency?"

5. Sales Strategist: "In your solo venture offering [specific product/service], you need a strong sales strategy. As the Sales Strategist, design a plan to identify leads, convert prospects, and close sales. What techniques will you use to track performance and optimize sales efforts?"

6. Web Developer: "You are building a one-person company with a focus on [specific service]. As the Web Developer, outline the key features and design elements for your website. How will you ensure user experience, SEO optimization, and effective call-to-actions?"

7. Product Manager: "In your new solo business providing [specific product], you are the Product Manager. Describe the process for developing and refining your product. What steps will you take for market research, product testing, and customer feedback integration?"

8. Graphic Designer: "For your one-person company specializing in [specific niche], you need visual branding. As the Graphic Designer, create a plan for your logo, business cards, and website graphics. How will you ensure a cohesive and professional visual identity?"

9. Operations Coordinator: "Running a solo business in [specific industry] requires smooth operations. As the Operations Coordinator, outline your daily, weekly, and monthly tasks. How will you manage inventory, suppliers, and administrative work efficiently?"

10. Legal Advisor: "As you launch a one-person business in [specific field], you need to address legal aspects. As the Legal Advisor, list the essential legal documents and agreements you need, such as contracts, terms of service, and privacy policies. How will you ensure compliance?"

11. Human Resources Manager: "Even as a solo entrepreneur in [specific area], you need HR strategies. As the HR Manager, describe your approach to managing your own workload, setting work hours, and maintaining a healthy work-life balance. How will you stay motivated and productive?"

12. Business Development Specialist: "In your new one-person company focusing on [specific market], you need growth strategies. As the Business Development Specialist, outline your approach for identifying new opportunities, partnerships, and markets. How will you prioritize and pursue these growth avenues?"

13. Social Media Manager: "Your solo business in [specific industry] needs a strong social media presence. As the Social Media Manager, create a detailed plan for content creation, engagement tactics, and analytics. How will you measure success and adapt your strategy?"

14. Customer Experience Designer: "For your one-person venture in [specific field], you want to enhance customer experience. As the Customer Experience Designer, map out the customer journey from first contact to post-purchase. How will you ensure a seamless and positive experience?"

15. Project Manager: "As the sole proprietor of a business specializing in [specific service], you need effective project management. As the Project Manager, describe how you will plan, execute, and monitor projects. What tools and techniques will you use to stay organized and meet deadlines?"

16. Advertising Specialist: "In your new one-person company focusing on [specific product/service], you need effective advertising. As the Advertising Specialist, develop a strategy for online and offline ads. How will you target your audience and measure the effectiveness of your campaigns?"

17. Tech Support Specialist: "Your solo business in [specific area] requires tech support for clients. As the Tech Support Specialist, draft a plan for handling technical issues, troubleshooting, and providing customer assistance. How will you ensure timely and effective support?"

18. Event Coordinator: "You are organizing events for your one-person business in [specific niche]. As the Event Coordinator, outline your process for planning, promoting, and executing events. What steps will you take to ensure successful and memorable events for your clients?"

19. Supply Chain Manager: "In your solo venture providing [specific product/service], managing supply chains is crucial. As the Supply Chain Manager, describe your approach to sourcing, inventory management, and logistics. How will you ensure efficiency and cost-effectiveness?"

20. Research Analyst: "Starting a one-person business in [specific field], you need thorough research. As the Research Analyst, develop a plan for conducting market research, competitor analysis, and industry trends. How will you use this information to make informed business decisions?"

Sure, here are 20 detailed prompts for creating a company of one, where ChatGPT takes on various job roles. Each prompt is designed to help someone start a small-scale digital business:

1. Business Idea Generation: "I need ChatGPT to brainstorm 10 unique business ideas for a digital company focusing on [industry/niche]. Each idea should include a brief description, target audience, and potential challenges."

2. Business Plan Development: "Please help me create a detailed business plan for my solo venture in [industry/niche]. Include sections on market analysis, revenue model, marketing strategy, and operational plan."

3. Brand Identity Creation: "ChatGPT, I need your help to develop a brand identity for my digital company named [Company Name]. Provide suggestions for logo design, color schemes, and brand voice that align with [specific values or message]."

4. Content Strategy: "Assist me in crafting a content strategy for my digital business. Outline a plan for blog posts, social media updates, and email newsletters that will engage my target audience of [target demographic]."

5. Website Development: "Guide me through the process of setting up a website for my digital business. Provide a checklist for essential pages, SEO optimization tips, and user experience best practices."

6. Product or Service Development: "Help me outline the steps to develop and launch a [digital product/service] for my company. Include ideation, prototyping, testing, and marketing strategies."

7. Sales Funnel Creation: "Create a detailed sales funnel plan for my digital business. Include lead generation tactics, email sequences, and conversion strategies tailored to [specific product/service]."

8. Customer Acquisition: "ChatGPT, provide a comprehensive plan for acquiring and retaining customers for my digital business. Include strategies for social media, paid advertising, and partnerships."

9. Financial Management: "Assist me in setting up a financial management system for my solo venture. Provide tips on budgeting, invoicing, tax planning, and tracking expenses."

10. Legal Considerations: "Help me navigate the legal aspects of starting a digital business. Include information on registering the company, intellectual property protection, and necessary contracts or agreements."

11. Marketing Plan: "Develop a detailed marketing plan for my digital business. Outline strategies for online advertising, SEO, content marketing, and public relations to reach [specific audience]."

12. Customer Service Strategy: "Create a customer service strategy for my digital company. Include guidelines for handling inquiries, complaints, and feedback, and suggest tools for efficient customer support."

13. Analytics and Metrics: "Guide me on how to set up analytics and track key performance metrics for my digital business. Focus on metrics related to website traffic, conversion rates, and customer engagement."

14. Networking and Partnerships: "Provide strategies for networking and forming partnerships that can benefit my digital business. Include tips for reaching out to potential partners and maintaining professional relationships."

15. Time Management: "Help me create a time management plan for running my solo digital business. Include strategies for prioritizing tasks, managing projects, and maintaining work-life balance."

16. Social Media Strategy: "Develop a comprehensive social media strategy for my digital business. Include recommendations for platform selection, content types, posting schedules, and engagement tactics."

17. Email Marketing Campaigns: "Create a plan for launching effective email marketing campaigns for my digital business. Include tips on list building, crafting compelling emails, and measuring campaign success."

18. Competitive Analysis: "Assist me in conducting a competitive analysis for my digital business. Identify key competitors, analyze their strengths and weaknesses, and suggest strategies to differentiate my company."

19. Customer Feedback Integration: "Help me develop a system for collecting and integrating customer feedback into my digital business. Include methods for gathering feedback, analyzing it, and implementing improvements."

20. Scalability Planning: "Guide me through the process of planning for scalability in my digital business. Include strategies for expanding product offerings, increasing market reach, and optimizing operations."

MORE PROMPTS

I'm going to share 2 blogposts written by Ali Abdaal. Analyze the blogposts and give me a set of instructions I can use to write in exactly the same tone, writing style, humor, reading level and delivery. Here are the blogposts:[Insert Post]

"I want to elevate my personal brand to 'oracle' status in Lyour industry]. First, ask me questions to learn more about my work. After that, help me develop a strategy to position myself as the go-to source for predictions, insights, and wisdom in my field. Suggest 5 unique ways I can demonstrate seemingly prophetic knowledge about industry trends and future developments. These methods should be attention-grabbing, slightly mystical, and reinforce my image as an unparalleled industry sage."

"Help me construct a compelling origin story for my personal brand. Here are key elements of my professional journey: [list 3-5 pivotal moments or experiences]. Create a narrative arc that highlights my transformation into an expert in [your field]. The story should be authentic, emotionally resonant, and clearly illustrate why I'm uniquely qualified to help my audience. Provide 3 different versions - one inspirational, one focused on overcoming adversity, and one that's more unconventional or surprising."

"Imagine I'm the go-to person in [your industry]. Your task is to reverse-engineer how I get there, taking inspiration from magnetic leaders. My goal is to create a personal brand so compelling that it naturally attracts my target audience and inspires them to follow my lead. Suggest 5 unconventional ways I can demonstrate my expertise and charisma to become an irresistible force in my field. These methods should be bold, slightly controversial, and impossible to ignore."

"Based on my experience in [your field] and my unique approach to [specific aspect of your work], help me develop a signature framework that I can use to explain my methodology to clients and audiences. This framework should have 3-5 key components, be easy to remember, and showcase my innovative thinking. Suggest 5 potential names for this framework and outline the core elements for each version."

"I work in [your industry/field] and my expertise lies in [your specific skills]. Help me identify a unique angle for my personal brand that will set me apart from others in my niche. Consider unconventional combinations of my skills, experiences, or perspectives. Provide 10 potential 'brand angles' that challenge the status quo and position me as a thought leader. For each angle, explain how it could differentiate me and attract my target audience."

"I'm planning a script for a [describe scenario, e.g. sales call or webinar] and I want to start with a story that describes the 'pinnacle of possibility. My audience is [describe your dream customer] and my product helps them [describe the outcomes you help them achieve.] Based on their deepest desires of [describe everything you know about these], create an off-the-cuff, relatable story I could tell at the start of my script, that helps them understand what they could achieve."

"As my company grows I want to make sure every team member feels like they can speak up about issues they see or improvements they want to make.
Specifically on the topic of [area of your business that is looked after by someone else], suggest 5 conversation starter questions that I can ask the team member responsible, in order to get their opinion. The questions should be inquisitive and open, not confrontational in any way."

"As my company grows I want to make sure my team and I don't forgo our health and happiness in pursuit of business success. Ask me a series of quiz-type questions, one by one, to ascertain my non-negotiables, for example if I'd skip a gym session to fulfill a last-minute client request. When I have answered 10 questions, suggest a series of 5 statements that outline the company non-negotiables. Ask me which I agree and disagree with until we have a final set of 5 that I will communicate with my team to get their input until we align."

"My company is growing and I want to continue to grow with it. Acting as a leadership coach, open a session where you ask me questions, one by one, to dig into the gaps in my leadership skills. Start with the question, What kind of leader do you aspire to be?' and continue the conversation to help me make a plan for improving."

"My company is growing and it's important that our values continue to shine through our work and not get lost or diluted as we add new people, products and processes. By analyzing my website's about page and other information about our company and who we serve, suggest 4 values pillars. For each one, name the value and explain how we will all work to maintain this value in everything we do at the company. [Paste your about page and other relevant information]"

"I want to streamline and automate the subscription management process for my business. This includes everything from billing to customer onboarding and delivery. Outline each process that I need to consider when offering and delivering this subscription. Ask me if I have a process, tool and/or person already in place to look after each one, then populate a table with this information and identify gaps where I need to take action to ensure the process is streamlined and automated where possible."
Understand

"I need to get a clear picture of the financials involved in my subscription business. Help me calculate the necessary subscription numbers and pricing to meet my financial goals. Ask me about my cost structure, desired profit margins, and current customer base size. Then, guide me through creating a model that estimates how many subscribers I would need at different price points to achieve profitability. This will help me set realistic prices and targets for my subscription service."

"I'm planning to test [specify which subscription concept you want to test] based on our previous discussions. The idea is to simulate a launch before fully committing, to see how potential subscribers react. Help me create a series of hypothetical customer scenarios and questions that I can use to gauge interest and collect detailed feedback on the subscription offer. Acting as a potential customer, ask questions that uncover what excites my ideal customer about the offer, any concerns they have, and their willingness to subscribe at the proposed price."

"I want to develop these ideas [choose your favourite ideas from the last section] into subscription offers.
For each one, we need to define the title, the components of the offer (what they get) as well as the price. Acting as a business consultant, ask me questions to collect information, then present each idea as a fully-fledged offer, making sure they will be irresistible to my ideal customer."

"My business is [describe your business], delivering [describe products or services] to help [describe your ideal customer] achieve [describe the outcome you help them achieve.] With that in mind, create 5 options for subscription-based products or services that they may want to buy, related to my business, that we could pivot to offering to make more revenue and delight our customers. Give each opportunity a name, then explain why it might be attractive to my ideal customers."

"My business is [describe your business] and my tasks include [describe the tasks in your role]. For each task, ask how this task is currently being completed and ascertain if this task could be automated. Once we identify tasks that might benefit from automation, create a 3-column table with these column headers: task, process now, process with automation. In column 2, outline these processes in detail and in column 3 create a plan for how each task could be automated. This structured approach will help me automate my business or prepare to work with an AI expert to implement time-saving automations."

"I want to maximize my productivity by aligning my tasks with my peak energy times using the law of least effort. Help me identify when I'm most effective and the types of tasks that best suit these high-energy periods. Start by asking me to list my activities from the past week and how energized I felt doing each one. Then, guide me through analyzing which tasks were most aligned with my peak times and which ones drained my energy. Ask questions such as, 'Which tasks did you complete most efficiently last week?' and 'During what times of day do you feel most energized to work?' Finally, help me plan a daily schedule that matches my most energy-efficient tasks with my natural productivity peaks, ensuring I perform optimally with minimal effort. This structured approach will help me maximize output while working in the most effortless way possible."

The prompt is simple: "Analyze the text below for style, voice, and tone. Create a prompt to write a new paragraph in the same style, voice, and tone." After adding your text, what follows will be the prompt that you can paste into future instructions to write in your style.

"Give me an inspirational pep talk focusing on self-forgiveness. I often overthink and blame myself when things don't go as planned, leading to [outcome, for example exhaustion and bad moods.] I'm working on being easier on myself, especially on acknowledging that it's okay to have off days. A recent example is [describe a specific situation where you've been hard on yourself recently]. Include advice that shifts my perspective to understand that challenging moments don't define my worth or capabilities. Guide me in embracing my reaction of [describe how you're wired or your typical reaction to stress] without harsh judgment, fostering a healthier, more compassionate approach to self-evaluation and growth."

"I have some doodles, notes, and lines I've jotted down in my notebook over the past few months. Transform my doodles into content ideas for my business, which [describe what your business does]. The social media platform I primarily use is [mention the platform].
Based on this information, help me develop these initial thoughts into engaging content ideas. The goal is to create posts that resonate with my audience of [describe your audience], that I can develop into fully fledged stories, posts, or campaigns."

"When I achieve success in my work, specifically [describe kind of success] I sometimes feel [describe the emotional response to success.] I want to ensure that this doesn't undermine my ability to be successful in the long term. Adopt the role of a personal development coach and ask me questions, one at a time, with the aim of building my sense of self-awareness so I can stay motivated and keep improving."

"Develop a concrete action plan based on the feedback I've received: [insert any recent feedback here]. I'm looking for ways to leverage this critique to enhance my [describe what to apply it to, for example strategies, products, or services.] Ask me clarifying questions, then suggest actionable steps or changes I can implement to transform this feedback into positive developments for my business, ensuring that I actively use it to improve my performance and outcomes."

Summarize the book [name of book] and cover all the important points mentioned.
Translate this piece of text into English [insert text].
Explain [insert topic] in simple and easy terms that any beginner can understand.

Write me a cover letter for my job hunting process [insert resume specifications/experience here].
Proofread my writing above. Fix grammar and spelling mistakes. And make suggestions to improve the clarity of my writing.

"My goal is to standardize a task. Your job is to help me create a streamlined process from this description, that I can give to a team member or easily follow in the future. Ask me questions to clarify any steps and suggest ways to simplify or automate the process. Once we have a clear process, add instructions to a team member to set up templates, write the rules, and save the instructions in an easily accessible location."

PROMPTS FOR WRITERS

Proofread this text for grammatical errors: [Insert Text Here]
Write a compelling product description for [Insert Product Name and Features Here]
Write a proposal for [insert Project or Proposal Details Here]
Write a 5-minute speech on the topic of [Insert Topic Here]
Write marketing copy for [Insert Product or Service Here]

PROMPTS FOR YOUR RESUME
Please review my resume and suggest improvements.
What are some common formatting mistakes to avoid in my resume?
How can I best highlight my achievements in my resume?
What can I do to make my resume stand out from other candidates?

PROMPTS FOR SALES
Generate 10 ways to generate leads for [product description]]
Create a personalized sales email for potential customers. Include [topic, brand name, promo offers, etc.]
Write a sales landing page description for [product description]
Generate 5 personas I should include in my outreach for [X]
Generate a script to use when cold-calling [insert persona]

PROMPTS FOR DEVELOPERS
Develop an architecture and code for a [website description] website with JavaScript.
Continue writing this code for JavaScript [post code].
Find the bug with in code: [post code).
Create a user journey for [insert app and persona description]
Generate UI/UX design requirements for [describe feature]

PROMPTS FOR EDUCATION

What are the most significant advancements in [topic]?
Discuss the history and development of [topic], its current applications and potential future impact.
Analyze the causes and consequences of the [event] and its influence on young adults today.
Explain the [topic] and give some examples.

PROMPTS FOR CONTENT CREATORS

Generate a creative social media content calendar for the next month for our [product].
Create a 2-minute video script for a Facebook ad campaign promoting [product or service].
Generate a list of 5 Linkedin articles to write for [topic].
Write a case study detailing [topic of choice].

HOW TO BUILD A CHAIN PROMPT WITH EXAMPLE
1. Insert first prompt: Give me a summary of this document [insert/copy paste document text]
2. Modify the output: Use the summary above and write a 500 word piece that explains to a fifth grader
3. Modify the tone: Change the tone of the answer above and make it sound more formal
4. Modify the format: Convert the answer above into text for a presentation with 1 slide for each key point

USING [x] tone
Formal
Objective
Confident
Descriptive
Poetic
Whimsical
Narrative
Academic
Assertive
Conversational
Informal
Friendly

MODES AND ROLES
Assistant: Find research on [insert topic]
Idea generator: Generate ideas on [x]
Proofreader: Proofread this [insert text]
Mentor: Guide me on [insert topic]
Critic: Critique my argument: [argument]

FORMAT
Table
Essay
Blog
Report
Email Presentation
List
Research

KEY USE CASES AND PROMPTS
Improve your writing: Proofread my writing above. Fix grammar and spelling mistakes. And make suggestions that will improve the clarity of my writing.

DELEGATE YOUR RESEARCH
I am creating a report about [insert topic]. Research and create an in-depth report with a step-by-step guide that will help readers understand how to [insert outcome].

LEARN NEW SKILLS
I want to learn [insert desired skill. Create a 30 day learning plan that will help a beginner like me learn and improve this skill.

USE 80/20 TO LEARN FASTER
I want to learn about [insert topic]. Identify and share the most important 20% of learnings from this topic that will help me understand 80% of it.

SUMMARIZE LONG TEXT, ARTICLES & REPORTS
Summarize the text below and give me a list of bullet points with key insights and the most important facts.

SIMPLIFY & UNDERSTAND COMPLEX DOCUMENTS
Rewrite this text and make it easy for a beginner to understand: [insert text].

GENERATE NEW IDEAS

I want to [insert task or goal]. Generate [insert desired outcome] for [insert task or goal].
Simplify and learn complex topics: Explain [insert topic] in simple and easy terms that any beginner can understand.

I'd like to make a short film that's between 60-90 seconds long. The concept of the film is that it will be a documentary about an AI robot that saves civilization. The film will have no dialogue. The entire film will have a voiceover narrator that tells the story. Please generate a script for the narrator to read that shares the story

"Describe a daily routine that incorporates exercise, healthy eating, and mindfulness practices. If needed, refine your answer to provide specific examples and a more detailed schedule."

"I have an interview for [enter position]. Provide a comprehensive list of questions I may be asked during this interview, along with concise answers to each one."

SPARK NEW IDEAS
"I aim to [insert task or goal]. Generate [insert desired outcome] for [insert task or goal]."

CHAPTER 7

SPECIALISED APPLICATION OF CHATGPT

ChatGPT's adaptability extends far beyond simple text generation and general-purpose conversations. By understanding and leveraging its advanced capabilities, you can apply ChatGPT to a range of specialized domains. Whether you are in education, healthcare, creative industries, or customer service, ChatGPT offers transformative potential that can be tailored to meet specific needs. This chapter delves into several specialized applications of ChatGPT, illustrating how this AI can be fine-tuned and integrated to serve distinct roles effectively.

EDUCATIONAL TOOLS AND TUTORING

ChatGPT can play a significant role in the educational sector by acting as a virtual tutor, providing personalized learning experiences, and aiding in content creation for educators.

Personalized Learning: Personalized learning is crucial for catering to diverse student needs and learning paces. ChatGPT can be configured to provide tailored responses based on individual student profiles, learning styles, and progress.

Adaptive Tutoring: ChatGPT can analyze a student's responses to quizzes and assignments to provide feedback and recommend resources tailored to their current understanding. For instance, if a student struggles with algebra, ChatGPT can offer additional practice problems and step-by-step explanations tailored to their specific difficulties.

Interactive Learning: ChatGPT can conduct interactive Q&A sessions, simulating a conversational tutor who can explain complex concepts, ask follow-up questions, and provide instant feedback. This interaction mimics a dialogue with a human tutor, making the learning process more engaging.

CONTENT CREATION FOR EDUCATORS

Teachers can use ChatGPT to streamline content creation, saving time and enhancing the quality of educational materials.

Lesson Plans: ChatGPT can generate comprehensive lesson plans based on specific topics, grade levels, and learning objectives. For example, a history teacher could ask ChatGPT to draft a week-long lesson plan on the Industrial Revolution, including key events, primary sources, and discussion questions.

Assessment Tools: ChatGPT can create diverse types of assessments, such as multiple-choice questions, essay prompts, and problem-solving exercises. These can be tailored to test different cognitive levels from knowledge recall to critical thinking.

Learning Resources: ChatGPT can summarize academic papers, generate explanatory diagrams, and create instructional videos scripts, helping educators present information in various formats to accommodate different learning preferences.

HEALTHCARE ASSISTANCE

In healthcare, ChatGPT's capabilities can be harnessed to support both patients and healthcare professionals by providing information, triaging symptoms, and facilitating communication.

Patient Interaction

ChatGPT can serve as a first point of contact for patients seeking medical advice or information, offering preliminary guidance and support.

Symptom Triage: By using symptom descriptions provided by patients, ChatGPT can offer preliminary assessments and suggest whether a visit to a healthcare professional is warranted. For example, if a patient describes symptoms of a cold, ChatGPT can differentiate between common cold and flu symptoms, providing advice on home care or recommending professional consultation.

Medication Information: ChatGPT can provide detailed information about medications, including usage instructions, potential side effects, and interactions with other drugs. This feature can enhance patient understanding and adherence to treatment plans.

PROFESSIONAL SUPPORT

Healthcare professionals can benefit from ChatGPT by using it as a tool for information retrieval, documentation, and patient education.

Information Retrieval: Doctors and nurses can use ChatGPT to quickly access medical literature, guidelines, and clinical trial results, aiding in evidence-based decision-making. For instance, a doctor could use ChatGPT to summarize the latest research on treatment options for hypertension.

Documentation Assistance: ChatGPT can assist in drafting patient notes, discharge summaries, and referral letters, reducing administrative burdens and allowing healthcare professionals to focus more on patient care.

Patient Education: ChatGPT can generate educational materials on various health conditions, treatment options, and preventive measures, which can be shared with patients to enhance their understanding and engagement in their health care.

CREATIVE WRITING AND CONTENT GENERATION

ChatGPT's ability to generate coherent and contextually relevant text makes it a powerful tool for creative writing and content generation in various media.

Storytelling and Scriptwriting

Writers can use ChatGPT to develop stories, scripts, and dialogues, exploring new creative possibilities and enhancing their writing process.

Plot Development: ChatGPT can suggest plot ideas, character arcs, and settings based on given prompts, helping writers brainstorm and overcome writer's block. For example, an author working on a science fiction novel could ask ChatGPT to develop a storyline involving time travel and parallel universes.

Dialogue Generation: ChatGPT can create dialogues between characters, capturing different tones and styles suitable for various genres. This can be particularly useful in scriptwriting for plays, movies, or video games, where realistic and engaging dialogues are crucial.

CONTENT CREATION FOR MEDIA AND MARKETING

Marketers and content creators can leverage ChatGPT to produce a wide range of content, from blog posts and social media updates to marketing copy and product descriptions.

Blog Posts: ChatGPT can generate well-structured blog posts on diverse topics, incorporating keywords and adhering to specific tone and style guidelines. For instance, a marketing team could use ChatGPT to create a series of blog posts on digital marketing trends and strategies.

Social Media Content: ChatGPT can draft engaging social media posts, headlines, and captions, tailored to different platforms and audiences. This can help maintain a consistent content schedule and enhance audience engagement.

Product Descriptions: ChatGPT can generate compelling product descriptions that highlight features, benefits, and use cases, enhancing the appeal and informativeness of e-commerce listings.

CUSTOMER SERVICE AND VIRTUAL ASSISTANCE

In customer service and virtual assistance, ChatGPT can automate responses, handle common queries, and provide a personalized customer experience.

Automated Customer Support

Businesses can deploy ChatGPT as a customer service agent to handle routine inquiries and support requests efficiently.

FAQ Automation: ChatGPT can answer frequently asked questions about products, services, policies, and technical issues. For example, a company could integrate ChatGPT into its website to handle questions about shipping policies, return procedures, and troubleshooting steps.

Ticket Triage: ChatGPT can categorize and prioritize customer support tickets, forwarding complex issues to human agents and resolving simpler ones automatically. This can streamline the support process and reduce response times.

Virtual Personal Assistants

Virtual personal assistants powered by ChatGPT can help users with scheduling, reminders, and task management, enhancing productivity and convenience.

Scheduling and Reminders: ChatGPT can manage calendars, schedule appointments, and send reminders, ensuring users stay organized and on top of their commitments. For instance, a virtual assistant could schedule a doctor's appointment and remind the user a day before the visit.

Task Automation: ChatGPT can assist with various tasks, such as booking travel, ordering supplies, or conducting online research, providing users with a hands-free experience for routine activities.

INTEGRATING CHATGPT WITH EXISTING SYSTEMS

To fully harness ChatGPT's potential in specialized applications, it is often necessary to integrate it with existing systems and workflows.

API Integration

ChatGPT can be integrated into various platforms and applications through APIs, allowing for seamless interaction with other systems.

CRM Systems: Integrate ChatGPT with Customer Relationship Management (CRM) systems to enhance data management, customer interaction, and sales processes. ChatGPT can help automate customer follow-ups, generate sales reports, and analyze customer feedback.

Learning Management Systems: Embed ChatGPT into Learning Management Systems (LMS) to provide on-demand tutoring, generate quizzes, and offer feedback on assignments, enhancing the e-learning experience.

Custom Plugins and Extensions

Developing custom plugins and extensions can tailor ChatGPT's functionalities to specific needs, improving its usability in niche applications.

Browser Extensions: Create extensions that allow users to access ChatGPT's capabilities directly from their browsers, such as summarizing articles, generating email drafts, or providing real-time translation.

IDE Plugins: Develop plugins for Integrated Development Environments (IDEs) that use ChatGPT to offer coding suggestions, error explanations, and documentation generation, enhancing the development workflow.

CHALLENGES AND CONSIDERATIONS

While ChatGPT offers significant benefits across various applications, there are challenges and considerations to keep in mind.

Ethical and Privacy Concerns

The deployment of ChatGPT must adhere to ethical guidelines and respect user privacy.

Data Privacy: Ensure that user data is handled securely and transparently, complying with data protection regulations such as GDPR or CCPA. Implement measures to anonymize sensitive information and seek user consent where necessary.

Bias and Fairness: Address potential biases in ChatGPT's responses by implementing fairness measures and regularly reviewing outputs for harmful or discriminatory content. This is crucial to prevent perpetuating stereotypes or misinformation.

Accuracy and Reliability

The accuracy and reliability of ChatGPT's responses can vary based on the complexity of the query and the specificity of the domain.

Verification: For critical applications, such as healthcare or legal advice, always verify ChatGPT's responses with authoritative sources. Use human oversight to ensure the information provided is accurate and reliable.

Continuous Improvement: Regularly update and refine ChatGPT's training data and configurations to enhance its performance and adapt to changing requirements. Incorporate feedback from users to identify and address areas for improvement.

ChatGPT's adaptability to specialized applications demonstrates its potential to transform various industries by enhancing automation, personalization, and interactivity. From education and healthcare to creative writing and customer service, ChatGPT can be customized to meet specific needs, providing significant value in diverse contexts.

As you explore these specialized applications, consider the ethical implications, ensure accuracy, and continuously refine your implementations to maximize the benefits of integrating ChatGPT into your workflows. This chapter highlights the broad scope of ChatGPT's capabilities, setting the stage for further innovation and practical application in your domain.

CHAPTER 8

ETHICAL CONSIDERATIONS AND CHALLENGES IN USING CHATGPT

The rise of advanced language models like ChatGPT presents exciting opportunities but also significant ethical challenges. As these models become more integrated into various facets of daily life, addressing ethical considerations becomes crucial to ensuring responsible and fair usage. This chapter explores the ethical dimensions of deploying ChatGPT, covering issues such as data privacy, bias, misinformation, accountability, and the broader social impact of AI technology. By understanding and addressing these ethical concerns, users and developers can navigate the complexities of AI with a greater sense of responsibility and integrity.

DATA PRIVACY AND SECURITY

Data privacy and security are paramount when using AI models like ChatGPT. The collection, processing, and storage of data can expose users to risks if not managed correctly.

Data Collection and Consent

When deploying ChatGPT, it is essential to be transparent about data collection practices and obtain user consent.

Transparency: Clearly inform users about what data is being collected, how it will be used, and who will have access to it. For example, a chatbot on an e-commerce website should disclose that it collects conversation data to improve customer service.

Consent Mechanisms: Implement mechanisms to obtain explicit user consent for data collection. This could include checkboxes in user interfaces or detailed privacy policies that users must agree to before interacting with ChatGPT.

Data Anonymization

Protecting user privacy involves anonymizing data to prevent identification of individuals from the information collected.

Anonymization Techniques: Use techniques such as data masking, tokenization, and aggregation to ensure that personal identifiers are removed from the data. For example, instead of storing full user names, replace them with pseudonyms or unique identifiers.

Re-identification Risks: Be aware of the risks of re-identification, where anonymized data can be cross-referenced with other datasets to reveal identities. Regularly assess and mitigate these risks to uphold user privacy.

DATA SECURITY

Securing the data used and generated by ChatGPT is critical to prevent unauthorized access and breaches.

Encryption: Implement robust encryption methods for data in transit and at rest. For instance, use TLS (Transport Layer Security) for data transmitted over the internet and AES (Advanced Encryption Standard) for stored data.

Access Controls: Establish strict access controls to limit who can view or modify data. Use role-based access controls (RBAC) to ensure that only authorized personnel have access to sensitive information.

Bias and Fairness

AI models like ChatGPT can inadvertently perpetuate biases present in their training data, leading to unfair or discriminatory outcomes.

UNDERSTANDING BIAS IN AI

Bias in AI can arise from various sources, including training data, model algorithms, and human oversight.

Training Data: If the training data reflects societal biases, the AI model may learn and reproduce these biases. For example, if a model is trained on biased text that stereotypes certain groups, it might generate outputs that reflect those stereotypes.

Algorithmic Bias: Even with unbiased data, algorithms can introduce biases through their structure or the way they process information. This can lead to disproportionate outcomes for certain groups.

Mitigating Bias

Efforts to mitigate bias involve strategies to identify, measure, and reduce bias in AI models.

Bias Detection: Implement tools and methodologies to detect bias in AI models. This can include analyzing the distribution of outputs across different demographic groups or testing the model with diverse inputs to observe disparities.

Bias Mitigation Techniques: Use techniques such as re-weighting training data, applying fairness constraints during model training, and post-processing adjustments to correct for biased outputs. For instance, re-weighting training examples to give more representation to minority groups can help reduce bias.

Continuous Monitoring: Regularly monitor and evaluate AI models to identify new biases as they arise. This ongoing process ensures that models remain fair and equitable over time.

ETHICAL REVIEW AND OVERSIGHT

Establishing ethical review boards and oversight mechanisms can help ensure that AI models are developed and deployed responsibly.

Ethical Review Boards: Create boards comprising ethicists, data scientists, and community representatives to review AI projects and provide guidance on ethical considerations. These boards can offer diverse perspectives and help navigate complex ethical dilemmas.

Accountability Frameworks: Develop frameworks for accountability that outline the responsibilities of developers, users, and organizations in mitigating bias and ensuring fairness. This includes establishing clear protocols for reporting and addressing ethical concerns.

Misinformation and Manipulation

AI models like ChatGPT have the potential to generate and spread misinformation, which can have serious societal consequences.

Risk of Misinformation

The ability of ChatGPT to generate coherent and believable text means it can be used to create misinformation, either intentionally or unintentionally.

Unintentional Misinformation: ChatGPT may generate incorrect or misleading information due to limitations in its training data or understanding. For instance, when asked about medical advice, it might produce responses based on outdated or incorrect information.

Intentional Manipulation: Malicious actors can exploit ChatGPT to create convincing fake news, propaganda, or deceptive content. This poses a risk of amplifying false narratives and misleading the public.

Combatting Misinformation

Addressing the spread of misinformation involves implementing safeguards and promoting responsible use of AI.

Fact-Checking Mechanisms: Integrate automated fact-checking tools to verify the accuracy of information generated by ChatGPT. These tools can cross-reference outputs with trusted sources to ensure reliability.

User Education: Educate users about the limitations of AI models and the importance of verifying information from multiple sources. For example, disclaimers can be added to AI-generated content to remind users to check the information.

Ethical Usage Policies: Develop and enforce policies that prohibit the use of ChatGPT for generating false or misleading information. These policies should outline acceptable use cases and consequences for misuse.

ACCOUNTABILITY AND TRANSPARENCY

Accountability and transparency are key principles in the ethical use of AI, ensuring that the deployment and outcomes of AI models are open to scrutiny and responsibility.

Explainability of AI Models

Explainability refers to the ability to understand and interpret the decisions and outputs of AI models.

Model Interpretability: Use techniques to make AI models more interpretable, such as highlighting the features or data points that influenced a particular output. For instance, in a medical diagnosis application, explainability tools can show which symptoms contributed most to the AI's diagnosis.

User Explanations: Provide clear explanations to users about how ChatGPT generates responses and the factors influencing its outputs. This transparency helps build trust and allows users to make informed decisions based on AI-generated content.

Responsibility for Outcomes

Ensuring responsibility for AI outcomes involves defining roles and responsibilities for the various stakeholders involved in developing and deploying AI.

Developers: Developers should be responsible for building and testing AI models to ensure they are ethical and fair. This includes conducting thorough evaluations and implementing safeguards against misuse.

Organizations: Organizations deploying ChatGPT should establish governance structures to oversee AI use, including ethical guidelines, compliance checks, and response mechanisms for ethical concerns.

Users: Users of AI models should be educated on responsible usage and encouraged to provide feedback on any ethical issues they encounter.

Audit and Compliance

Regular audits and compliance checks help ensure that AI models adhere to ethical standards and regulatory requirements.

Ethical Audits: Conduct ethical audits to review AI models and their deployment practices. These audits can assess aspects such as bias, fairness, and privacy, providing recommendations for improvement.

Regulatory Compliance: Ensure that the use of ChatGPT complies with relevant regulations and standards, such as data protection laws and AI ethics guidelines. Regular compliance checks can help maintain adherence to legal and ethical requirements.

BROADER SOCIAL IMPACT

The deployment of AI models like ChatGPT has broader social implications that extend beyond individual use cases, affecting societal structures and interactions.

Impact on Employment

AI automation can disrupt job markets, potentially leading to job displacement while also creating new opportunities.

Job Displacement: As AI models automate tasks traditionally performed by humans, there is a risk of job displacement, particularly in roles involving repetitive or routine tasks. For example, customer service roles may be impacted by AI-powered chatbots.

New Opportunities: Conversely, AI can create new job opportunities in fields such as AI development, data analysis, and AI ethics. It can also augment human roles by handling routine tasks, allowing workers to focus on more complex and creative activities.

Equity and Access

Ensuring equitable access to AI technology is crucial to prevent exacerbating existing social inequalities.

Digital Divide: The benefits of AI should be accessible to diverse populations, including those in underserved or marginalized communities. Efforts to bridge the digital divide can include providing affordable access to AI tools and investing in digital literacy programs.

Inclusive Development: Engage diverse communities in the development and deployment of AI to ensure that the technology meets the needs of different groups. This can involve participatory design processes and community consultations.

Cultural and Ethical Considerations

AI deployment should be sensitive to cultural and ethical contexts, respecting local norms and values.

Cultural Sensitivity: AI models should be developed and deployed in ways that respect cultural differences and avoid reinforcing harmful stereotypes. This can involve incorporating diverse perspectives and data sources into AI development.

Ethical Alignment: Ensure that AI applications align with ethical principles, such as fairness, autonomy, and beneficence. This alignment can guide the development of AI models that are ethically sound and socially responsible.

Navigating the ethical considerations and challenges of using ChatGPT requires a comprehensive approach that addresses data privacy, bias, misinformation, accountability, and

 the broader social impact of AI. By implementing robust safeguards, promoting transparency, and fostering responsible usage, stakeholders can leverage ChatGPT's capabilities while mitigating potential ethical risks.

As AI technology continues to evolve, ongoing dialogue and proactive measures are essential to ensure that its benefits are realized in a way that is ethical, fair, and inclusive. This chapter underscores the importance of ethical considerations in AI deployment, providing a foundation for responsible and sustainable AI practices.

CHAPTER 9

CONCLUSION

———————————

AI ChatGPT Essentials: From Novice to Expert is a comprehensive guide designed to meet the needs of both beginners and experienced users interested in understanding and utilizing AI-powered tools like ChatGPT. As artificial intelligence rapidly transforms many facets of modern life, tools like ChatGPT have become increasingly relevant in various industries, including creative writing, education, customer service, and technical support. Yet, understanding how to engage effectively with these systems is critical to unlocking their full potential. This book fills that gap by providing a structured, step-by-step approach that not only introduces foundational AI concepts but also delves into more advanced and nuanced applications.

One of the most significant challenges for newcomers to AI is understanding how it works and how to engage with it meaningfully. ChatGPT is a prime example of an AI-driven tool that, on the surface, may appear simple to use, but its capabilities are far more extensive than casual interactions might suggest. AI ChatGPT Essentials takes the reader from the basics—like defining what AI and machine learning are— through to the more sophisticated techniques required to maximize ChatGPT's functionality. The book's structured progression ensures that by the time readers reach the advanced sections, they have already developed a solid grounding in AI theory, making it easier to comprehend and apply complex ideas.

Importance of User Input in AI Interaction

One of the key elements emphasized in the book is the role of user input in shaping the behavior and output of AI systems like ChatGPT. In AI-powered conversations, the quality of the input directly influences the quality of the response. AI, particularly language models like ChatGPT, relies on textual cues to generate meaningful and relevant responses. For users new to this kind of interaction, this may not be immediately obvious. AI ChatGPT Essentials offers valuable insights into how users can craft tailored prompts to guide the AI towards producing accurate, helpful, and contextually relevant answers.

A poorly structured query or ambiguous prompt can lead to vague or incorrect responses, while a precise and well-thought-out question can elicit detailed, insightful answers. This point cannot be overstated—crafting prompts is an art that requires practice, and this book provides numerous examples and exercises to help users refine their approach. Through these examples, readers gain an appreciation for how AI 'thinks' and how they can guide the system to deliver optimal results for specific use cases, whether it's generating creative content, answering technical queries, or even simulating human-like conversations.

Refining the Interaction

Understanding how to refine AI interactions is another crucial skill that AI ChatGPT Essentials addresses. While initial input is important, the iterative process of interacting with AI also plays a significant role in achieving the desired outcome. As readers progress through the book, they learn techniques for refining conversations, tweaking prompts, and following up with additional queries to clarify or expand on the AI's responses. This continuous feedback loop between user and machine allows for more dynamic and useful exchanges, especially in complex scenarios where the AI might need additional context to provide accurate information.

The refinement process also helps users avoid common pitfalls, such as overloading the AI with too much information at once or asking overly broad questions that can confuse the system. By breaking down tasks and guiding the AI step by step, users can make ChatGPT more effective and efficient. This level of interaction refinement is critical in professional settings, where precision and reliability are often required, such as in drafting business documents, generating code, or assisting with research.

Ethical Implications and Responsible AI Usage

AI ChatGPT Essentials also emphasizes the importance of understanding the ethical implications of AI usage. As AI becomes more integrated into daily life, issues related to bias, fairness, and transparency are growing concerns. While AI can provide tremendous benefits, it also has the potential to perpetuate harmful biases if not used responsibly. This is particularly true with language models like ChatGPT, which are trained on vast amounts of internet data that may include biased or harmful content.

The book addresses these ethical concerns by educating readers on how to identify potential biases in AI responses and how to mitigate them. Additionally, it emphasizes the importance of using AI in a way that is respectful of privacy and personal data. As AI continues to evolve and influence more areas of life, the responsible use of these tools will become increasingly significant. AI ChatGPT Essentials offers practical advice on how to navigate these issues, encouraging readers to not only think critically about their own interactions with AI but also consider the broader societal implications of widespread AI adoption.

AI ChatGPT Essentials positions ChatGPT not only as a tool for personal or professional use but as a window into the future of AI-driven innovation. The book highlights the many potential applications of ChatGPT across different fields and industries. For example, educators can use AI to generate lesson plans or assist students with research, while businesses can implement AI-driven customer service solutions to improve efficiency and response times. Creative professionals, such as writers, musicians, and artists, can harness the AI's capabilities to break through creative blocks or generate novel ideas.

The book's discussion of ChatGPT's potential applications demonstrates that AI tools are becoming increasingly accessible and versatile. The ability to use AI effectively will open up new opportunities for innovation, allowing individuals and businesses to streamline their processes, enhance creativity, and offer more personalized services. As more people become proficient in interacting with AI tools, we can expect to see even more exciting developments on the horizon.

Ultimately, AI ChatGPT Essentials serves as a roadmap for anyone looking to leverage the power of ChatGPT effectively. By making AI more accessible, the book demystifies complex technologies and encourages users to explore the full potential of AI-driven systems. Whether readers are engaging with AI for creative projects, professional endeavors, or personal interest, they will find the tools and techniques necessary to make the most of ChatGPT.

As AI continues to evolve, those who understand its intricacies and applications will be better positioned to take advantage of the opportunities it offers. AI ChatGPT Essentials provides the foundational knowledge and practical skills necessary to navigate this exciting and rapidly changing field. The guide's emphasis on ethical AI usage ensures that readers not only harness the power of AI but do so in a way that is responsible and forward-thinking, setting the stage for a future where AI plays an even more integral role in our daily lives.

CHAPTER 10

FUTURE DIRECTIONS AND INNOVATIONS IN CHATGPT

As artificial intelligence continues to advance at an unprecedented pace, the future of ChatGPT and similar large language models promises to be both exciting and transformative. The evolution of these technologies will likely focus on enhancing capabilities, addressing current limitations, and exploring novel applications.

This chapter provides a comprehensive exploration of potential future directions for ChatGPT, considering advancements in model architecture, integration with emerging technologies, ethical considerations, and the broader societal impacts. By anticipating these developments, we can better prepare for a future where AI plays an even more integral role in our lives.

ADVANCEMENTS IN MODEL ARCHITECTURE

Future advancements in ChatGPT's architecture are expected to enhance its performance, scalability, and adaptability to various tasks and contexts.

Scaling Model Size and Efficiency

One major trend in AI development is the scaling of model size to increase performance. However, this comes with challenges related to efficiency and resource consumption.

Larger Models: Scaling up model size can improve performance on complex tasks by capturing more nuanced patterns in data. Future versions of ChatGPT could incorporate billions or even trillions of parameters, leading to more sophisticated understanding and generation capabilities.

Efficient Architectures: Balancing model size with efficiency is crucial to manage computational costs and environmental impact. Innovations in model compression, such as distillation and pruning, and new architectures like sparsity-based models can help achieve this balance.

These techniques allow for maintaining or even enhancing performance while reducing the computational load.

Specialized Architectures

Developing specialized architectures tailored to specific domains or tasks can enhance ChatGPT's applicability and performance in those areas.

Domain-Specific Models: Creating variants of ChatGPT that are fine-tuned for specific domains, such as medicine, law, or finance, can improve the accuracy and relevance of its responses in these contexts. For instance, a medical-specific version of ChatGPT could integrate domain knowledge and terminology to provide more accurate diagnostic suggestions and treatment options.

Multimodal Models: Integrating text with other data modalities, such as images, audio, and video, can enable ChatGPT to understand and generate content across different formats. For example, a multimodal version of ChatGPT could analyze a video's content and generate a summary or respond to queries about the visual elements.

Interactive and Context-Aware Models

Enhancing ChatGPT's ability to maintain context over longer interactions and understand more complex conversational dynamics is a key area of future research.

Contextual Memory: Developing mechanisms to maintain and retrieve contextual information across extended conversations can improve the coherence and relevance of responses. Future models might employ advanced memory networks or hierarchical attention mechanisms to achieve this.

Personalization: Incorporating personalization features that adapt responses based on individual user preferences, histories, and behaviors can make interactions with ChatGPT more engaging and useful. This could involve techniques like user profiling and adaptive learning algorithms.

INTEGRATION WITH EMERGING TECHNOLOGIES

The future of ChatGPT involves integration with a range of emerging technologies, enhancing its capabilities and expanding its application scope.

AI and Internet of Things (IoT)

Integrating ChatGPT with IoT devices can enable smarter, more responsive environments by combining natural language processing with real-time data from connected devices.

Smart Homes: ChatGPT can be embedded in smart home systems to facilitate natural language interaction with various devices, such as thermostats, lights, and security systems. For example, users could issue complex voice commands to their smart home assistants to adjust settings or retrieve information.

Industrial IoT: In industrial settings, ChatGPT can assist in monitoring and managing equipment by interpreting data from sensors and providing insights or control suggestions based on natural language queries.

AUGMENTED REALITY (AR) AND VIRTUAL REALITY (VR)

The convergence of ChatGPT with AR and VR technologies can create immersive, interactive experiences across education, gaming, and professional training.

Immersive Learning: In educational contexts, ChatGPT integrated with AR/VR can provide interactive tutoring sessions, simulations, and virtual field trips, enhancing engagement and learning outcomes. For instance, students could explore a virtual ancient city while receiving real-time historical commentary from ChatGPT.

Virtual Assistants: In VR environments, ChatGPT can serve as a virtual assistant, offering guidance, explanations, or interactive narratives within the virtual space. This can enhance user experiences in gaming, virtual conferences, or online collaborative workspaces.

Blockchain and Decentralized Technologies

The integration of ChatGPT with blockchain technology can enhance transparency, security, and trust in AI interactions and data management.

Data Integrity: Using blockchain for data storage and transaction logs can ensure the integrity and transparency of interactions with ChatGPT. This can be particularly valuable in applications requiring high levels of trust, such as financial transactions or legal advice.

Decentralized AI: Deploying ChatGPT in decentralized frameworks can distribute computational resources and data across a network, potentially reducing the reliance on centralized servers and enhancing privacy and security.

ETHICAL AND REGULATORY CHALLENGES

As ChatGPT evolves, addressing ethical and regulatory challenges will be crucial to ensure responsible development and deployment.

Ethical AI Development

Future advancements in ChatGPT must prioritize ethical considerations to mitigate risks and promote fairness.

Bias Mitigation: Ongoing research and development efforts will focus on advanced techniques for identifying and mitigating bias in AI models. This could include more sophisticated fairness algorithms and comprehensive datasets that reflect diverse populations and contexts.

Transparency and Explainability: Enhancing the transparency and explainability of AI models will be key to building trust and accountability. Future ChatGPT versions might incorporate features that allow users to understand the rationale behind its responses more clearly.

Regulatory Compliance

Adapting to evolving regulatory landscapes will be essential for the lawful and ethical use of ChatGPT.

Data Protection Laws: Compliance with data protection regulations such as GDPR, CCPA, and future AI-specific laws will remain a critical focus. This involves ensuring that ChatGPT's data handling practices align with legal requirements and respect user rights.

AI Governance: The development of AI governance frameworks and standards will help guide the responsible deployment of ChatGPT. These frameworks may include guidelines on ethical use, transparency, and accountability, and could be informed by multi-stakeholder collaborations.

Broader Societal Impacts

The widespread adoption of ChatGPT will have significant implications for society, influencing various aspects of daily life and human interactions.

Impact on Employment and Skills

The integration of ChatGPT into diverse workflows will transform job markets and skill requirements.

Job Transformation: While AI automation may replace certain roles, it will also create new opportunities and shift the focus towards more creative, analytical, and complex tasks. Workers will need to adapt by acquiring new skills and leveraging AI as a tool for enhanced productivity.

Reskilling and Education: The demand for reskilling and continuous learning will increase as AI becomes more prevalent in the workplace. Educational institutions and training programs will need to evolve to provide the necessary skills and knowledge for the AI-driven economy.

Human-AI Collaboration

Future interactions between humans and AI will likely emphasize collaboration, where AI augments human capabilities rather than replacing them.

Enhanced Decision-Making: ChatGPT can assist in decision-making processes by providing insights, recommendations, and data analysis, enabling humans to make more informed and effective decisions. For example, in healthcare, ChatGPT could support doctors by analyzing patient data and suggesting potential diagnoses or treatment options.

Creative Partnerships: In creative industries, ChatGPT can act as a collaborator, generating ideas, content, and solutions that inspire and complement human creativity. This collaborative dynamic can lead to innovative outcomes in areas such as writing, design, and art.

Digital Inclusion and Equity

Ensuring that the benefits of ChatGPT are accessible to all segments of society will be a critical goal.

Bridging the Digital Divide: Efforts to make AI tools like ChatGPT accessible to underserved and marginalized communities will be essential to promote digital inclusion and equity. This includes providing affordable access, language support, and tailored interfaces for diverse user groups.

Empowering Communities: Community-driven initiatives and participatory design approaches can help ensure that AI solutions meet the needs and aspirations of different communities, empowering them to leverage AI for positive social impact.

Research and Development Horizons

The future of ChatGPT will be shaped by ongoing research and development in AI and related fields.

Next-Generation Language Models

Research into next-generation language models will focus on achieving more human-like understanding and interaction capabilities.

Grounded Understanding: Future models may incorporate grounding techniques to better understand context and background knowledge, leading to more accurate and contextually appropriate responses. This involves integrating world knowledge and situational awareness into the language model.

Interactive Learning: Innovations in interactive learning will enable models to learn from user interactions in real-time, adapting to new information and evolving user needs dynamically. This can enhance the responsiveness and personalization of AI interactions.

Collaborative AI Research

Collaborative research efforts will play a crucial role in advancing AI technology and addressing its challenges.

Open Research Initiatives: Open research initiatives and collaborative platforms will facilitate the sharing of knowledge, data, and tools among researchers, promoting innovation and addressing common challenges. This can lead to more rapid advancements in AI capabilities and applications.

Ethical AI Research: Collaborative efforts to develop ethical AI research frameworks will help ensure that advancements in AI align with societal values and ethical principles. This includes interdisciplinary collaborations involving ethicists, technologists, and policymakers.

The future of ChatGPT is poised to be dynamic and impactful, driven by advancements in model architecture, integration with emerging technologies, and a strong focus on ethical considerations. As ChatGPT continues to evolve, it will shape the way we interact with technology, make decisions, and collaborate in both personal and professional settings. Anticipating these future directions involves not only technical advancements but also ethical foresight and societal preparedness.

ETHICAL FORESIGHT AND SOCIETAL PREPAREDNESS

Preparing for the future of ChatGPT requires proactive measures to address ethical concerns and ensure that its benefits are equitably distributed.
Ethical Considerations in AI Development

Continued efforts to embed ethics into AI development will be essential to mitigate risks and promote responsible AI use.

Human-Centered Design: Adopting human-centered design principles ensures that AI technologies like ChatGPT are developed with user well-being and societal impact in mind. This involves involving diverse stakeholders in the design process and prioritizing user feedback.

Ethics by Design: Incorporating ethics into the design phase involves identifying potential risks, such as bias and privacy concerns, and integrating safeguards and accountability mechanisms from the outset. This proactive approach can help prevent ethical issues from arising later in deployment.

Societal Impact Assessments

Conducting impact assessments can help anticipate and mitigate potential social implications of ChatGPT deployment.

Social Impact Analysis: Assessing how ChatGPT deployment may impact employment, education, healthcare, and other sectors enables proactive measures to maximize benefits and minimize risks. For example, identifying opportunities for job creation in AI-related fields can inform workforce development initiatives.

Community Engagement: Engaging with communities affected by AI deployment fosters trust, transparency, and accountability. This can involve public consultations, community forums, and participatory decision-making processes to ensure that AI technologies align with community values and priorities.

POLICY AND REGULATORY FRAMEWORKS

Developing robust policy and regulatory frameworks will be crucial to govern the responsible use of ChatGPT and other AI technologies.

AI Governance and Regulation

Establishing clear guidelines and regulations can ensure that AI technologies are deployed ethically and in compliance with legal standards.

AI Ethics Guidelines: Developing comprehensive AI ethics guidelines that outline principles, best practices, and compliance requirements helps organizations navigate ethical dilemmas and promote responsible AI use. These guidelines can be informed by international standards and adapted to local regulatory contexts.

Regulatory Compliance: Enforcing regulations such as data protection laws, consumer rights, and AI-specific regulations ensures that ChatGPT deployment respects user privacy and upholds ethical standards. Regulatory bodies play a crucial role in monitoring compliance and enforcing penalties for non-compliance.

International Collaboration

Promoting international collaboration and coordination facilitates the development of harmonized AI governance frameworks.

Global Standards: Establishing global standards for AI development and deployment fosters consistency and interoperability across borders. This includes agreements on data sharing, interoperability of AI systems, and ethical guidelines that transcend national boundaries.

Multilateral Partnerships: Collaborating with international organizations, governments, and industry stakeholders enables knowledge sharing, capacity building, and coordinated responses to global AI challenges. This collaborative approach ensures that AI technologies benefit societies worldwide while respecting cultural diversity and local contexts.

Educational and Research Initiatives

Investing in education and research initiatives prepares individuals and institutions to harness the full potential of ChatGPT and AI technologies.

AI Education and Literacy

Promoting AI literacy and skills development equips individuals with the knowledge and capabilities to engage with ChatGPT effectively.

Curriculum Integration: Introducing AI education into school curricula at an early age cultivates digital literacy, critical thinking, and ethical reasoning. This prepares future generations to navigate AI technologies responsibly and innovatively.

Continuing Education: Offering training programs, workshops, and certifications in AI enables professionals to upskill and adapt to evolving AI landscapes. Continuous learning ensures that individuals can leverage ChatGPT and other AI tools effectively in their careers.

Research and Innovation

Supporting research and innovation in AI drives advancements in ChatGPT capabilities, applications, and ethical frameworks.

Funding Initiatives: Investing in AI research funding supports breakthrough discoveries, interdisciplinary collaborations, and the development of cutting-edge technologies. This accelerates progress towards more intelligent, reliable, and ethical AI systems.

Open Access to Data and Tools: Promoting open access to AI datasets, tools, and research findings facilitates collaboration and innovation among researchers worldwide. This democratizes AI development and promotes inclusivity in the AI community.

COLLABORATION AND STAKEHOLDER ENGAGEMENT

Collaboration among stakeholders is essential for shaping the future of ChatGPT in a way that benefits society as a whole.

Public-Private Partnerships

Engaging public and private sectors in collaborative efforts maximizes the impact and effectiveness of ChatGPT deployment.

Industry Collaboration: Partnering with industry leaders fosters innovation, accelerates technology adoption, and ensures that ChatGPT meets market demands and industry standards. This collaboration can drive real-world applications in diverse sectors, from healthcare to finance.

Academic Partnerships: Collaborating with universities and research institutions promotes knowledge exchange, research excellence, and talent development in AI. Joint initiatives in AI ethics, responsible AI deployment, and technology transfer enhance the societal impact of ChatGPT research and development.

Community and Civil Society Engagement

Involving civil society organizations, advocacy groups, and community stakeholders ensures that ChatGPT deployment reflects diverse perspectives and societal values.

Partnering with civil society organizations strengthens advocacy efforts for AI ethics, privacy rights, and equitable access to AI technologies. This collaboration promotes transparency, accountability, and social responsibility in ChatGPT deployment.

Conducting outreach programs and awareness campaigns educates the public about AI technologies, their benefits, and potential risks. Engaging with communities builds trust, addresses concerns, and fosters informed dialogue on the ethical use of ChatGPT.

The future of ChatGPT holds immense promise for transforming industries, enhancing user experiences, and advancing societal well-being. By embracing ethical principles, investing in research and education, and fostering collaboration among stakeholders, we can navigate the opportunities and challenges of ChatGPT deployment responsibly.

Anticipating future advancements in model architecture, integration with emerging technologies, and ethical governance frameworks prepares us to harness the full potential of ChatGPT while safeguarding human values and societal interests.

ABOUT THE AUTHOR

DR. OBRUCHE ORUGBO, PhD.

Obruche is a seasoned expert in the field of User Experience (UX) design and research, whose extensive background informs his writing in "AI ChatGPT Essentials - From Novice to Expert." With over seven years of professional experience and a PhD in Human-Computer Interaction (HCI) from the University of Sunderland, Obruche has established himself as a leading voice in the UX consultancy landscape.
His approach combines theoretical knowledge with practical application, allowing readers to navigate the complexities of AI technology effectively.

Currently, Obruche is the founder of xploreUX, a consultancy dedicated to delivering bespoke UX solutions. His work involves deep dives into user behaviors through Discovery User Research and Rapid UXR services. His comprehensive methodology includes Expert UX Reviews and Website

Audits, which provide invaluable insights for organizations looking to enhance their digital products. Obruche's commitment to aligning UX strategy with business objectives ensures that his clients not only meet user needs but also achieve their organizational goals.

In addition to his consultancy work, Obruche serves as a UX researcher with now-u, where he employs various research methodologies to gather and analyze user insights. His ability to communicate findings effectively has fostered dynamic collaboration across multifunctional teams, making him a critical asset in any project he undertakes.

Obruche's academic journey laid the groundwork for his current expertise. He completed his PhD research in 2023, focusing on improving usability evaluation methods to aid UX practitioners and designers. His academic endeavors also include a Master's degree in Information Technology Management, where he conducted significant research on the application of classification techniques for online platforms.

Through his role as a part-time educator at the University of Sunderland, Obruche marks and facilitates online learning, contributing to the next generation of computer science students. His dedication to teaching and mentorship reflects his belief in the importance of sharing knowledge and empowering others in the field.

Obruche has also consulted for various organizations, enhancing their products through rigorous user research and usability testing. His ability to conduct stakeholder interviews and develop user personas showcases his understanding of the multifaceted nature of UX design, particularly in industries such as healthcare, finance, and e-commerce.

Beyond his consultancy and academic roles, Obruche actively engages with the UX community. His volunteer work at events like the UX Live Conference exemplifies his commitment to fostering connections within the industry and staying abreast of the latest trends and best practices.

"AI ChatGPT Essentials - From Novice to Expert" is not just a technical manual; it is a reflection of Obruche's passion for making complex technologies accessible and practical. Through this book, he aims to guide readers from a basic understanding of AI to a level of expertise that enables them to leverage these powerful tools in their own contexts. His rich blend of experience, education, and commitment to user-centered design positions him uniquely to help others thrive in the evolving landscape of AI and UX.

GLOSSARY

Glossary of 100 AI-related terms:

---

1. Algorithm: A set of rules or instructions for solving a problem or performing a task.

2. Artificial Intelligence (AI): The simulation of human intelligence in machines programmed to think and learn.

3. Machine Learning (ML): A subset of AI that allows systems to learn from data and improve over time without being explicitly programmed.

4. Deep Learning: A specialized form of ML that uses neural networks with many layers to analyze various factors of data.

5. Neural Network: A computational model inspired by the human brain, consisting of interconnected nodes (neurons).

6. Natural Language Processing (NLP): The branch of AI that focuses on the interaction between computers and humans through natural language.

7. Computer Vision: A field of AI that enables machines to interpret and understand visual information from the world.

8. Supervised Learning: A type of ML where the model is trained on labeled data.

9. Unsupervised Learning: A type of ML where the model is trained on unlabeled data, identifying patterns on its own.

10. Reinforcement Learning: A type of ML where an agent learns by interacting with its environment and receiving rewards or penalties.

11. Training Data: The dataset used to train a model in ML.

12. Validation Data: A subset of data used to evaluate the performance of a model during training.

13. Test Data: Data used to assess the model's performance after it has been trained.

14. Overfitting: When a model learns the training data too well, including noise, resulting in poor generalization to new data.

15. Underfitting: When a model is too simple to capture the underlying pattern of the data.

16. Feature: An individual measurable property or characteristic of the data used in ML models.

17. Label: The output variable in supervised learning, representing the result we want the model to predict.

18. Loss Function: A method of evaluating how well a model's predictions match the actual results, guiding the learning process.

19. Gradient Descent: An optimization algorithm used to minimize the loss function by iteratively adjusting model parameters.

20. Epoch: One complete pass through the entire training dataset during the training process.

21. Batch Size: The number of training examples used in one iteration of model training.

22. Hyperparameters: Configurable parameters that are set before training, affecting the learning process.

23. Activation Function: A mathematical function that determines the output of a neuron in a neural network.

24. Convolutional Neural Network (CNN): A type of deep learning model primarily used for processing grid-like data, such as images.

25. Recurrent Neural Network (RNN): A type of neural network designed for sequential data, allowing information to persist.

26. Transfer Learning: A technique where a pre-trained model is fine-tuned on a new but related task.

27. Generative Adversarial Network (GAN): A framework where two neural networks compete, one generating data and the other evaluating it.

28. Explainable AI (XAI): AI systems designed to provide human-understandable insights into their decision-making processes.

29. Bias: Systematic error in a model due to assumptions made in the learning algorithm.

30. Dataset: A collection of data used for training, validating, or testing a model.

31. Semantic Analysis: The process of understanding the meaning and context of words in text.

32. Tokenization: The process of breaking down text into smaller units (tokens) for analysis in NLP.

33. Chatbot: An AI program designed to simulate conversation with human users.

34. Voice Recognition: Technology that converts spoken language into text.

35. Recommendation System: An AI system that suggests products or content to users based on their preferences.

36. Anomaly Detection: Identifying unusual patterns that do not conform to expected behavior in data.

37. Data Mining: The practice of examining large datasets to discover patterns and extract valuable information.

38. Artificial Neural Network (ANN): A computational model based on the structure and function of the brain, used in machine learning.

39. Robotics: The intersection of AI and engineering, focusing on the design and creation of robots.

40. Autonomous Systems: Machines that can perform tasks without human intervention.

41. Natural Language Generation (NLG): The process of generating human-like text from structured data.

42. Computer-Aided Design (CAD): Software that enables designers to create precision drawings or technical illustrations.

43. Simulated Annealing: A probabilistic technique for approximating the global optimum of a given function.

44. Support Vector Machine (SVM): A supervised ML algorithm used for classification tasks.

45. Feature Engineering: The process of selecting, modifying, or creating features to improve model performance.

46. Data Augmentation: Techniques used to increase the diversity of training data without collecting new data.

47. Text Classification: The process of categorizing text into predefined labels.

48. Clustering: A type of unsupervised learning that groups similar data points together.

49. Dimensionality Reduction: Techniques to reduce the number of features in a dataset while preserving important information.

50. Self-supervised Learning: A form of ML where the model learns from unlabeled data by predicting parts of the input from other parts.

51. Knowledge Graph: A structured representation of knowledge that connects entities and their relationships.

52. Semantic Web: An extension of the web that allows data to be shared and reused across applications.

53. Ensemble Learning: Techniques that combine multiple models to improve overall performance.

54. Bayesian Networks: Probabilistic graphical models that represent a set of variables and their conditional dependencies.

55. Multi-task Learning: A learning approach where a model is trained on multiple tasks simultaneously.

56. Predictive Analytics: The practice of using data, statistical algorithms, and ML techniques to identify future outcomes.

57. Edge Computing: Processing data near the source of data generation rather than relying on a central data center.

58. Data Privacy: Protecting personal information from unauthorized access and misuse.

59. Federated Learning: A decentralized approach to training ML models where data remains on local devices.

60. Synthetic Data: Data generated artificially rather than obtained from real-world events.

61. Turing Test: A test for determining whether a machine can exhibit intelligent behavior indistinguishable from a human.

62. ChatGPT: A conversational AI model developed by OpenAI that can engage in dialogue with users.

63. OpenAI: An AI research organization focused on developing and promoting friendly AI.

64. AI Ethics: The study of moral implications and responsibilities associated with AI technologies.

65. Robustness: The ability of a model to perform well under varying conditions and inputs.

66. Data Pipeline: A series of data processing steps to collect, transform, and load data for analysis.

67. A/B Testing: A method of comparing two versions of a webpage or app against each other to determine which performs better.

68. Scalability: The capacity of a system to handle growing amounts of work or data.

69. Crowdsourcing: Obtaining input or data from a large group of people, often via the internet.

70. Game Theory: A mathematical framework for modeling scenarios in which conflicts of interest exist.

71. Feature Selection: The process of selecting a subset of relevant features for model training.

72. Cognitive Computing: Simulating human thought processes in a computerized model.

73. Intelligent Automation: The use of AI to automate complex business processes.

74. Data Scientist: A professional who uses data analysis and modeling to extract insights and inform decision-making.

75. Ethical AI: The practice of developing AI systems that adhere to ethical standards and values.

76. Knowledge Representation: The way information and knowledge are structured and stored in AI systems.

77. Sentiment Analysis: The computational task of determining the emotional tone behind a series of words.

78. Zero-shot Learning: The ability of a model to recognize objects or concepts it has never seen before.

79. Augmented Reality (AR): An interactive experience where real-world environments are enhanced with computer-generated information.

80. Virtual Reality (VR): A simulated experience that can be similar to or completely different from the real world.

81. Contextual AI: AI systems that can understand and interpret the context of data and interactions.

82. Adaptive Learning: Systems that adapt their learning strategies based on user interactions and performance.

83. Human-in-the-loop: A model where human feedback is integrated into the AI learning process.

84. MLOps: Practices that combine ML system development and operations to automate and streamline the deployment of ML models.

85. Explainability: The degree to which an AI model's actions can be understood by humans.

86. Chatbot Framework: A software framework that facilitates the development of chatbots.

87. Data Sovereignty: The concept that data is subject to the laws and governance structures within the nation it is collected.

88. Information Retrieval: The process of obtaining information system resources that are relevant to an information need.

89. Neural Architecture Search: The process of automating the design of neural networks.

90. Smart Contracts: Self-executing contracts with the terms of the agreement directly written into code

91. Data Governance: The management of data availability, usability, integrity, and security.

92. Human-Computer Interaction (HCI): The study of how people interact with computers and to design technologies that let humans interact with computers in novel ways.

93. Predictive Maintenance: Techniques to predict when equipment will fail to allow for planned maintenance.

94. Digital Twin: A digital representation of a physical object or system used to simulate, predict, and optimize performance.

95. ChatGPT API: An application programming interface that allows developers to integrate ChatGPT capabilities into their applications.

96. Behavioral Cloning: A method in ML where the model learns by mimicking the behavior of an expert.

97. Data Scientist vs. Data Analyst: Data scientists focus on advanced analytics and predictive modeling, while data analysts typically handle data processing and reporting.

98. AI-Generated Content: Content created by AI systems, including text, images, or music.

99. Neural Machine Translation (NMT): A type of machine translation that uses deep learning models to translate text from one language to another.

100. Robustness Testing: Evaluating how well a model performs under various conditions, including adversarial attacks or unexpected input.

REFERENCE

Appendix: Resources and Further Reading

Allen, D., 2023. How to Use AI Prompts to Plan Custom Lessons Fast. The English Connection, p.26.

Bansal, G., Chamola, V., Hussain, A., Guizani, M. and Niyato, D., 2024. Transforming conversations with AI—a comprehensive study of ChatGPT. Cognitive Computation, pp.1-24.

Baracchini, F. and Stary, C., 2023. „What is the Impact of ChatGPT on Facilitating Knowledge Provision and Creation? Examples and Criticalities in Classroom Education ". In Proceedings International Conference on Knowledge Management ICKM (Vol. 23).

Chakraborty, U., Roy, S. and Kumar, S., 2023. Rise of Generative AI and ChatGPT: Understand how Generative AI and ChatGPT are transforming and reshaping the business world (English Edition). BPB Publications.

Chandrasekar, R., 2014. Elementary? Question answering, IBM's Watson, and the Jeopardy! challenge. Resonance, 19(3), pp.222-241.

Chang, H.S., Fu, M.C., Hu, J. and Marcus, S.I., 2016. Google DeepMind's AlphaGo: operations research's unheralded role in the path-breaking achievement. Or/Ms Today, 43(5), pp.24-30.

Chen, J., Lu, X., Du, Y., Rejtig, M., Bagley, R., Horn, M. and Wilensky, U., 2024, May. Learning agent-based modeling with LLM companions: Experiences of novices and experts using ChatGPT & NetLogo chat. In Proceedings of the CHI Conference on Human Factors in Computing Systems (pp. 1-18).

Cordeschi, R., 2007. AI turns fifty: revisiting its origins. Applied Artificial Intelligence, 21(4-5), pp.259-279.

Davis, R.O. and Lee, Y.J., 2023. Prompt: Chatgpt, create my course, please!. Education Sciences, 14(1), p.24.

Gupta, N., Choudhuri, S.S., Hamsavath, P.N. and Varghese, A., 2024. Fundamentals Of Chat GPT For Beginners Using AI. Academic Guru Publishing House.

Hammer, E., 2024. ChatGPT in the Classroom: The Teacher's Challenges and Opportunities in an AI Revolution.

Hassani, H. and Silva, E.S., 2023. The role of ChatGPT in data science: how ai-assisted conversational interfaces are revolutionizing the field. Big data and cognitive computing, 7(2), p.62.

Joyner, D.A., 2024. A Teacher's Guide to Conversational AI: Enhancing Assessment, Instruction, and Curriculum with Chatbots. Taylor & Francis.

Moor, J.H., 1976. An analysis of the Turing test. Philosophical Studies, 30(4), pp.249-257.

McCulloch, Warren S., and Walter Pitts. "A logical calculus of the ideas immanent in nervous activity." The bulletin of mathematical biophysics 5 (1943): 115-133.

Newborn, M. and Newborn, M., 2003. Deep Blue: an artificial intelligence milestone. Springer Science & Business Media.

Opara, E., Mfon-Ette Theresa, A. and Aduke, T.C., 2023. ChatGPT for teaching, learning and research: Prospects and challenges. Opara Emmanuel Chinonso, Adalikwu Mfon-Ette

Theresa, Tolorunleke Caroline Aduke (2023). ChatGPT for Teaching, Learning and Research: Prospects and Challenges. Glob Acad J Humanit Soc Sci, 5.
Sharma, N.K., Maurya, S.K. and Kapoor, P.A., 2024. Navigating the Future: Trends and Applications in Artificial Intelligence and Machine Learning. In Harnessing Artificial Emotional Intelligence for Improved Human-Computer Interactions (pp. 1-12). IGI Global.

Sidiropoulos, D. and Anagnostopoulos, C.N., 2024, June. Applications, Challenges and Early Assessment of AI and ChatGPT in Education. In International Conference on Breaking Barriers with Generative Intelligence (pp. 1-12). Cham: Springer Nature Switzerland.

Styve, A., Virkki, O.T. and Naeem, U., 2024, May. Developing Critical Thinking Practices Interwoven with Generative AI Usage in an Introductory Programming Course. In 2024 IEEE Global Engineering Education Conference (EDUCON) (pp. 01-08). IEEE.

van den Berg, G. and du Plessis, E., 2023. ChatGPT and generative AI: Possibilities for its contribution to lesson planning, critical thinking and openness in teacher education. Education Sciences, 13(10), p.998.

Wang, K.D., Burkholder, E., Wieman, C., Salehi, S. and Haber, N., 2024, January. Examining the potential and pitfalls of ChatGPT in science and engineering problem-solving.

In Frontiers in Education (Vol. 8, p. 1330486). Frontiers Media SA.

Weizenbaum, J., 1966. ELIZA—a computer program for the study of natural language communication between man and machine. Communications of the ACM, 9(1), pp.36-45.

Printed in Great Britain
by Amazon

48106628R00126